Haena State Beach, Kauai

Island Style

On the Island, we do it Island Style,
From the mountain to the ocean from
the windward to the leeward side.

Mama's in the kitchen cooking
dinner real nice,
Beef stew on the stove,
lomi salmon with the ice.
We eat and drink and we sing all day,
Kanikapila in the old Hawaiian way.

On the Island, we do it Island Style,
From the mountain to the ocean from
the windward to the leeward side.

We go grandma's house on the
weekend clean yard.
If we no go, grandma gotta work hard.
You know my grandma,
she like the poi real sour.
I love my grandma every minute,
every hour.

On the Island, we do it Island Style,
From the mountain to the ocean from
the windward to the leeward side.

lyrics by John Cruz

John's new album,
One of These Days,
was released in 2007

A *Trailblazer* TRAVEL BOOK

NO WORRIES HAWAII
A VACATION PLANNING GUIDE FOR
KAUA'I, OAHU, MAUI, AND THE BIG ISLAND

FIRST EDITION, REVISED THIRD PRINTING

TEXT BY JERRY SPROUT
PHOTOGRAPHS, ART DIRECTION & DESIGN BY JANINE SPROUT
TECHNICAL CONSULTATION BY MICHAEL SAGUES

For Bijou, Mica, Tundra, Bridger, Sophie, Luke, Carson, Chloe, Richie, Lola, Jack, Pal, Smokey Joe Brown, Coco Sam, JJ, Pike, Solano, Tracker King, Chester, Frankie, Bill, Brows, Shag, Rainbow, Dexter, Tiny, Sunshine, Nikki, Lulu, Zizi, Nina, Jake, Kena, Shila, Josie, Aspen, and Hailey.

With special thanks to our Trailblazer ohana: Jimmy Dunn and Paula Pennington, John and Patty Brissenden, John and Suzanne Barr, Gregory Hayes and Joan Wright, Richard and Kathryn Ann Zellars Harvey, Jack and Sandy Lewin, Joseph Stroud and Ellen Scott, Rob Moser, Mark P. and Vicki Hyde, John Manzolati and Linda Kearney, Jim Rowley and Carol Mallory, Judy Farnsworth, Barbara and Gary Howard, Elsa Kendall, the Michael Sagues family, the Matthew Sagues family, and the Rickfords, Derek, Anna, Collin, Holly, Owen, Dane and Katie.

DIAMOND VALLEY COMPANY
Publishers of Trailblazer Travel Books

89 Lower Manzanita Drive, Markleeville, CA 96120
Post Office Box 422, Kilauea, HI 96754
www.trailblazertravelbooks.com
trailblazertravelbooks@gmail.com

ISBN-10: 0-9670072-9-1
ISBN-13: 978-0-9670072-9-8
Library of Congress Catalogue card number 2007902765

Proofreader: Greg Hayes
Cover: Lagoon at Anahola Bay, Kaua'i
Back cover: Waianae

A Vacation Planning Guide for
Kaua'i, Oahu, Maui, and the Big Island

Jerry and Janine Sprout

A Trailblazer Travel Book
DIAMOND VALLEY COMPANY, PUBLISHERS
MARKLEEVILLE, CA | KILAUEA, HI

Hanalei Bay, Kauaʻi

NO WORRIES HAWAII is an offering to
all people working to preserve the natural
beauty and cultural traditions of Hawaii.

Mahalo Nui to the people who have shared their aloha:

Donald Bodine; Roberta and Gordon Haas; Diane Gardner; Bob Keane; Jerry and Sarah Dow; Chuck DiPiazza at Air Kauai; Fred Atkins and Pepe Trask; Franchesa the glass lady; Francis in Kealia; Melinda Morey; Elaine and Marionette; Sue Kanoho, Kauai Visitors Bureau; Dave and Kristen Alred; Kalani Kali; David Boyntan; Tarey Low, Department of Land and Natural Resources; Frederick Wichman; Kim Olivier at Captain Andy's; Titus Kinimaka; Freckles Smith in Wailea; Dawn Traina; Lani Kawahara, Hawaii State Public Library; Fred and Carol Tangalin; Kaleo Ho'okano, Water Safety Supervisor; Mary Requilman, Kaua'i Historical Society; Linda Monroe; Edwin O. Hagstrom; Beth Tokioka, Public Information Officer; Paulette Burtner at Koke'e Museum; Keala Senkus, Hularoom; Diane Ferry, Kinipopo Gallery; Janet Leopold and Phyllis Segawa, Allerton Gardens; Lillian de Mello, Kapa'a Camera Club; Chipper, Phyllis Crain, and Annella at Limahuli Tropical Garden; Chris Faye at Gay & Robinson; Doug and Sandy McMaster at Ki Koalu; Denise Carswell at Princeville Ranch; Joe and Lihue Kimimaka-Lopez, Margaret and Dennis Daniels; Tiane, David, and Cole Cleveland at Wailua River Kayak;

Miguel Salmoiraghi; Les and Loraine Miller; Barbara and Gary Anderson at the Shipman House, Lorna and Albert at Kilauea Lodge, Dave Griffin at Blue Hawaiian, Jan and Tim Gillespie; Michael Tuttle at Hawaii's Best Bed & Breakfast, Daniel Kaniela and Anna Akaka, Donna Saiki Pacific Tsunami Museum, David Nardin at the Mauna Loa Observatory, Keoki at the Mauna Lani Resort; Laura Craft at the Keck Observatory, Mauna Kea; Gary Rothfus; Albert Kehaulani Solomon Jr. at Kamuela Museum; Gil Kaheli at Miloli'i; Nancy and Greg Gerard; Nalani and Moira at Hawi Post Office; Edie Paulson and Timothy Pemberton; John Kitchen et. al. at Hawaii Forest & Trail; Kia and Patty McCarthy in Wapio Valley; Grace Dehmer at Akaka Café; Aunty Lei at the Waikoloa Marriott; Loni Kuhl at the Four Seasons; Lily Anne and Lele at Kaloko Historical Park; Mervin et al. at Ho'okena Beach Park; Seishi at UCC coffee in Kealekekua; Jan and Frank Morgan, Kohala Bookshop; Wayne Subica, Memories of Hawaii; Yumi at Maokupapa'a Center; Marsha Hee at Volcano Art Center; Larry at White Sands Beach Park; Janet and Sean at Hawaii Tropical Botanical Garden; Caleb at Kaupulehu Cultural Center; Kumu Nani Yim Lap; Bo and Patrick at Kalopa State Park; Jeff the security guy at Kona Village; Paul Gephardt at Hawaii Artifacts; Lynne Kreinberg at Kealia Ranch Store; Suga' Daddy; Jack Johnson; Bianca Soriano and Emory Aceret, Halau Na Pua 'O Uluhaimalama; Brittney Dinson;

'Haleiwa' Jane Duncan and Greg Koop; William Kaihe'ekai Maiolho at the Royal Mausoleum; Alma Watene and Crease at Kavaroots Bonecarving; Buffalo and the Keaulana family of Makaha; Anne Wharton, Shaun Chillingworth of Bishop Museum; Maria Borgess at Iolani Palace; Charlie Aldinger, Honolulu Academy of Art; Jean at the Hawaii Maritime Center; B.J. Whitman, Moana Surfrider; The late Dino Ching at Kuhio Beach Park; Mark Heckman at the Waikiki Aquarium; Martha Yent and Aaron Lowe at the Department of Land and Natural Resources; Kalani at the Hawaii Nature Center; Donna Schultz at Lyon Arboretum; Max and Doug at HURL; Olive Vanselow, Ho'omaluhia Botanical Garden; Will Ho, Honolulu Park & Recreation; David Morgan at Kualoa Ranch; Emma at Tropical Farms; Shiela at Kahana Valley; Sister Ian at the Mormon Temple; Charlie Silva at the Turtle Bay Resort; Hazel and Aunty Kaula at Waimea Valley Audubon Center; Steven Gould at the North Shore Surf Museum; Floren Elman at Hawaii's Plantation Village; Keith Awai at the Polynesian Cultural Center; Brian Melzack at Bestsellers; Winnie Singeo at Foster Garden; Charles Hinman, Bowfin Submarine Museum; Chuck Battles, Camp Timberline; Steve Mayher, Ko'olau Golf Club; James Ho, Hawaiian Chinese Museum; Maura Jordan at Oahu Visitors Bureau; Emma at Tropical Farms; Teresa at Hawaiian Railway Society; Arthur Wong, Arnold, Will Ho at City and County of Honolulu; Anuhea Rodrigues Auld;

Marsha at Maui Visitors Bureau; Lucienne de Naie, Maui Tomorrow; Joseph W. Bean; Larry Rodriques et al at Baldwin Beach; Marian Feenstra at Department of Parks and Recreation; Steve Knight, Captain Andy at Island Marine; Dave Castles at Maui Dive Shop; Robert at Hotel Lanai; Dexter Tom at Department of Land & Natural Resources; Becky at Haleakala National Park; Aunty Sarah at Kai Pali Place; Jerry at Hawaiian Islands Humpback Whale Sanctuary; Melissa Kirkendall, State Historic Preservation Division; Russell Sparks, Division of Aquatic Resources; Kate Zolezzi at Maui Ocean Center; ; June Friewald, Pacific Whale Foundation; Ka'au Abraham, Humpback Marine Sanctuary; Jason Coloma at Swinging Bridges; Ali'i Chang at Maui Kula Lavender; Paula Heggle Tedeschi Vineyard; Sandy and Tammy Hueu from Keanae; Leimomi at Hotel Hana Maui; J.D. Wyatt at Hawaii Nature Center; Linda Domen at Kaupo Store; surfer Dan Moore; photographer Frank Quirarte; Roslyn Lightfoot, Maui Natural History Association; and many other fellow travelers on the beaches, trails, and back roads of Hawaii.

Part Three: THE ELEMENTS OF ISLAND STYLE
What to do, and not to do, when you get to Hawaii

Part Four: THE BEST OF HAWAII

Part Five: WIKIWIKI PHONEBOOK

NO WORRIES HAWAII is for people who have never been to the islands and for returnees who want to try something new. Use this book both to plan the details of your trip and as a checklist of the best stuff to do when you arrive.

Begin at the beginning, and read your way through each part:

Part One – THE ARMCHAIR VOYAGE. In Part One, you build the vacation of your imagination. First, take a self-administered test that guides you to select the island, or islands, that are right for you and your travel mates. Then, review the different locales in the islands —from the little grass shack to a destination resort—and find one that fits your style and budget. Finally, make a choice on how much time you want to allot on an island, based on what you want to get out of the visit.

Part Two – DA PLAN! THE PLAN! You begin Part Two knowing which island to visit, what there is to do there, how long you'll want to stay, and in what locale. In Part Two, it's time to make it happen. You'll need specific lodging (or perhaps more than one), airline tickets, probably a rental car, and a suitcase full of personal possessions. Part Two explains how to find an accommodation that will make you happy. You will get advice on how to save time and money when booking airline passage and a rental car.

Part Three – THE ELEMENTS OF ISLAND STYLE. Although you should read this section before your visit, Part Three is about what to do—and what not to do—once you set foot in the islands. You'll get advice on how to plan your day and how to map out a vacation to get maximum enjoyment with minimum hassle.

In Part Three, you'll also find out which tours and activities (like cruises, surfing lessons, horseback rides) give the most bang for the buck—and how to book them conveniently and economically. Included also are a host of ways to save money without scrimping on enjoyment. A must-read section is the safety tips—how to avoid hazards that can torpedo the best-planned vacation.

Part Four—BEST OF HAWAII CATEGORY WINNERS—At the heart of this book are the BEST OF categories, which list what's best to see and do on the island. You'll find all the best—beaches, trails, snorkeling and surfing, parks, tourist towns, museums, visitor centers, attractions—listed for each island and covering 36 categories.

Part Five—WIKIWIKI PHONEBOOK—Gives the specific contact numbers and recommendations for travel brokers, accommodations, outfitters and tour guides, attractions, museums, public agencies and parks, and visitor information.

NO WORRIES HAWAII is a companion book to Diamond Valley Company's Trailblazer Travel Books. These books include more than 1,000 recreational activities and attractions, with 36 maps, and some 900 photographs—much more than could be put into this planning guide. Each island guide gives directions, descriptions, and historical backgrounds for all the activities referenced in No Worries Hawaii—plus many more that didn't make the cut.

But you don't need to buy these books, or any others, to have fun on your vacation. If you're on a short stay and want to hit just the better-known highlights, you can get by using free tourist publications that are available at kiosks throughout the islands. However, a number of activities in No Worries Hawaii will not be listed in other publications or books, except the following:

KAUAI TRAILBLAZER
Where to Hike, Snorkel, Bike, Paddle, Surf

MAUI TRAILBLAZER
Where to Hike, Snorkel, Paddle, Surf, Drive

HAWAII THE BIG ISLAND TRAILBLAZER
Where to Hike, Snorkel, Surf, Bike, Drive

OAHU TRAILBLAZER
Where to Hike, Snorkel, Surf
From Honolulu to the North Shore

Hookipa windsurfer, Maui; Waikaloa petroglyph, fern, and lava flow. Big Island

PART ONE

The Armchair Voyage

Boiling Pots, Wailuku River State Park, Big Island

FIRST TAKE THE JOURNEY IN YOUR MIND

PART ONE

WHY HAWAII?

You can find white-sand beaches, aquamarine pools, fruity cocktails, and swaying palms at many wonderful places on this big blue orb. People debate which destination is best, and Hawaii gets many votes. But aside from being the tropical fantasy, what makes Hawaii unequaled, no ifs ands or buts? Here are Ten Big Truths, and one exaggeration, that apply to Hawaii—and only to Hawaii.

1. THE LAST LOST WORLD

Human beings had inhabited virtually the entire world before migrating to Hawaii. The earliest known footprints were made about 200 AD by sailing canoe voyagers from the Marquesas, coming some 2,400 miles from the south. A second wave of voyagers, from Tahiti, arrived around 1200 AD. These Polynesians—the Hawaiians—made back-and-forth migrations for several centuries, until the late 1400s, when they were isolated on their Pacific homeland

2. THE NEWEST NEW WORLD

The Western World, in the form of British Captain James Cook (who was looking for the Northwest Passage) found Hawaii only recently—in 1778. These islands in the Pacific became crucial to expanding trans-Pacific trade. At that time, the Hawaiian population was thought to be around 600,000. Sixty years later, due to the outbreak of Western diseases, native Hawaiians numbered about 50,000.

3. THE WORLD'S HOTTEST HOT SPOT

The Hawaiian Islands are volcanoes. Although the northernmost main island, Kaua'i, is more than 5 million years old, parts of the Big Island are as fresh as a newborn babe. That's because the earth's crust is slowly moving northward over a "hot spot" of copiously flowing magma, like the shell of an egg rotating around its yoke. New lava piles up and forms islands, and then the islands move north. Loihi, the newest would-be island, is now underwater about 20 miles offshore the Big Island.

4. NOW YOU SEE 'EM, NOW YOU DON'T

As the islands move forward on the geologic conveyor belt, they are eroded by rain, wind, and waves. The Hawaiian Islands include more than 100 tiny islands and sea-washed atolls north of Kaua'i. Kaua'i is headed for submersion, to be followed by the other islands. (Five million years ago, Kaua'i was 10,000 feet higher, and located about where the Big Island is today.)

5. THE WORLD'S TALLEST MOUNTAINS

True, the Big Island's volcanoes, Mauna Loa and Mauna Kea, are just under 14,000 feet in elevation. But if you measure from their peaks to the base on the seafloor, they are around 40,000 feet—easily the earth's tallest.

6. BIGGEST STATE IN THE UNION

That's right Texas, you're number three. The Hawaiian Archipelago extends for about 1,600 miles and contains some 123 islands, all comprising the State of Hawaii. If territorial waters are included in area, the total is more than twice the size of Alaska.

7. FARTHEST GETAWAY IN THE WORLD

The eight major Hawaiian Islands are in the middle of the Pacific, surrounded by 65-million square miles of open water and at least 2,000 miles from other islands or continents. It's easily the world's most isolated landmass. You want a getaway, this is it.

8. THE ORIGIN OF SPAM

Sure, everybody with email knows about spam now. But Spam is all about Hawaii, where record amounts are enjoyed each year per person. The craze began when Hawaiian warriors in ancient times sailed north into the Pacific, harboring pigs in open canoes as was their custom. Reaching the Mainland, they then paddled up the Colorado River, scaled the Grand Canyon, crossed the Great Plains, and reached the frozen tundra of Austin, Minnesota. The pigs could go no far-

Why Hawaii cont'd—

ther. Absent ti leaves for a luau, the Hawaiians concocted a way to jellify the pork into square cans. During WWII, Hormel Foods started shipping the stuff back to Hawaii.

9. THE ORIGIN OF NEW LIFE FORMS

Some 6,000 insects, birds, and plants are native to the Hawaiian Islands, having evolved from about 120 seeds that washed up or were flown here in bird stomachs. Hawaii became rich with endangered and rare species, many of which are now extinct. An isolated Eden, a planet in the Pacific, Hawaii is where new earth rises from the sea and new life forms evolve. The Polynesians brought new species to their island home, and thousands of exotic plants have since been introduced.

10. WETTEST SPOT ON EARTH

Mount Waialeale on Kaua'i gets some 40 feet of rainfall per year, and several other locations on all the islands receive 25 feet or more. Rainfall is not normally a selling point for vacation destinations. But all that rain translates to resplendent greenery and waterfalls. Most of the rain takes place at the highest elevations inland. The leeward sides of the islands are desertlike, complete with cacti, receiving around 10 inches of rain reach year.

11. ALOHA LIVES

Led by transplanted Americans, a rebellion of business interests overthrew the Hawaiian Kingdom in 1893, later imprisoning Queen Liliuokalani in her own palace. President Grover Cleveland at the time ruled the overthrow illegal and that the monarchy be restored. But his ruling was ignored, and when McKinley took office in 1898, the islands were annexed as a U.S. territory. Since Queen Liliuokalani chose to combat the overthrow in the courts rather than on the battlefield, the legal issue of Hawaii's sovereignty remains an open question. The U.S. formally apologized for the overthrow in 1993. The unmet promise of the Hawaiian Kingdom remains an open issue and aloha—Hawaii's export to a world in need—remains a hope unfulfilled. If you look, you will see the spirit of aloha, not preserved for tourists, but rather living and breathing in the people and traditions of Hawaii.

Lanikai Beach, Oahu

A FLING OR A MEANINGFUL RELATIONSHIP?
Pick a vacation style that best fits you and your travel mates

Let's say Hawaii has captured your imagination and you'd like to go. Before selecting an island and where to stay, you should decide what kind of vacation you want—your vacation style. You'll also want to factor in who is going with you and their styles. Is it a solo journey of discovery? A relaxing getaway for a two? A family vacation? A reunion? An adventure safari among roommates? Your vacation style, and that of your travel mates, will determine what island is best to visit and what locale will be right for you and your group.

THE THREE STYLES OF HAWAIIAN VACATIONS

A FLING

If your aim is to see what the islands are about—perhaps a scouting expedition for next time—then we'll call that a Fling. A fling will be an exciting overview. Flings involve the logistics of moving around between accommodations, lots of sightseeing scheduling, and driving tours. Flings are best for solo travelers or intimate companions, since flings involve stop-and-go decisions, which are cumbersome for groups. Ironically, flings are often the style of larger groups, whose members are marching to a schedule that everyone has seen before departure and which is overseen by a leader.

Visitors looking for a fling are likely to have a large number and a wide range of Gotta-Have-It requirements; they want to see and do it all, but not focus in on one area. Locale will not be as important for flings, since people are out and about during the day, and perhaps switching locales during the vacation. At the end of a fling, you will have a sense of accomplishment for having completed the journey, with plans to revisit your favorite spots. TIME NEEDED: From 4 to 16 days: (4 days, including jet travel, for one island; or 2 to 4 days per island for up to 4 islands.)

A ROMANTIC INTERLUDE

If you need a break from life in a beautiful place for R&R, then we'll call that a Romantic Interlude. Romantic interludes are about you—taking some time off and indulging in self-pampering, self-healing. Group size doesn't matter so much in a romantic interlude, so long as people in the group have the freedom to answer personal musings about how to spend time. Family reunions and smaller groups usually want this type of vacation. A Romantic Interlude can be had in as little as a week, long enough to soak in Hawaii and let your body recuperate—as well as time to take a day trip or two from the hotel to hit the island's highlights. But a two-week romantic interlude is optimum.

Visitors seeking a romantic interlude are likely to have fewer Gotta-Have-It requirements. The attributes of your locale, and your specific accommodation, will be more important than the scope of the entire island. People will be hanging around the resort, and groups will splinter into smaller groups for different activities. You'll want to pay attention to what is available close to your chosen locale. After a Romantic Interlude, you're likely to return home sated, rested, and ready get back to business. TIME NEEDED: One to two weeks.

A MEANINGFUL RELATIONSHIP

If you want to explore a new place and have outdoor adventures with a sense of self-improvement, then you're looking for a Meaningful Relationship. In the span of two weeks or more you can shed your skin, feel the aloha, and perhaps charter a new course for your life. You won't run out of things to do, if you are a curious and active visitor. Group size can vary in a meaningful relationship, as long as everyone is on the same page, but that is not easily accomplished. Couples and solo travelers will be most likely to enjoy this type of vacation.

Those seeking a meaningful relationship will have a larger number of Gotta-Have-It require-

Three Styles of Vacations cont'd—

ments, but they will tend to focus in on an area of interest, say, hiking and visiting cultural sites, or some other combination of a few categories. Accommodations and locale will not be as important for Meaningful Relationships, since visitors are often out from dawn to dusk (though where you stay always matters). After a Meaningful Relationship, you're apt to return home satisfied, but exhausted, perhaps inspired to make positive changes in your life. TIME NEEDED: Two to four weeks.

Of course, flings can develop into a romantic interlude, and romantic interludes can be part meaningful relationship. Good Lord, what you thought was a meaningful relationship may turn out to have been a fling. The point is, you can mix-and-match the styles, balancing out the days to suit your inclinations.

Waikiki from Diamond Head

A SELF-TEST TO PICK YOUR ISLAND—OR ISLANDS

Now that you've decided to go to Hawaii and have thought about your vacation style, the question becomes, which island? More than one island?

Begin the self-test ... by finding a piece of paper. Write two column headings side by side: one labeled "Gotta Have It," and the other "Would Be Nice." Leave room below these headings.

Step One
GOTTA HAVE IT
Look over the 36 Best Of categories, enumerated on pages 16 and 17. (For harmonious results, everyone who's going to Hawaii in your group should review the categories.) As you find a category you "gotta have" (really want) on your Hawaiian vacation, write the number for that category below your Gotta-Have-It heading. Be selective. These are your babies. But then again, don't be afraid to pile on in certain areas, say, all the different categories in swimming, if that's a primary interest. You are not looking for balance, necessarily.

Step Two
WOULD BE NICE
After everyone has reviewed the Best Of categories and written down their numbers, review the categories again. This time look for things that

"would be nice" to do on your visit, and write those category numbers below the Would-Be-Nice heading. You may want to do these things, but you're not sure and want to see if you have time. Be selective again, but be aware that some of Hawaii's charms may be foreign to you, so don't be afraid to follow your fancy. Today's Would-Be-Nice may be tomorrow's Gotta-Have. (The Best Of categories left out of your selections comprise your Don't Care list, and you shouldn't.)

Step Three
KEEP SCORE
Now go to the meat of the Best Of Scorecard on page 66. Find out which island "wins" each of your chosen Gotta-Have-It categories. Write the initial for that island next to the corresponding number on your Gotta-Have-It list. For a few categories, there will be co-winners. In these

cases write both islands' initials under the heading. Then do the same thing for Would-Be-Nice choices. Record the initial of the island(s) that wins the category.

AND THE WINNER IS ...
Your pick among the islands is the one that has the most Gotta-Have-It winners. Use the Would-Be-Nice to weight the result if the decision is close. Also, use the close-seconds to sway your decision. (To determine second-place islands, go to the category results page, as noted on the

Scorecard, and see how each island stacks up.) If after all this, you wind up with a "tie," you might decide to visit two islands, or more. Keep in mind that this self-test is a way to objectify what is a subjective opinion, so don't be too rigid when looking at your test results.

Step Four
ARGUE ABOUT THE RESULTS
It will be good practice for making decisions when you actually do get to Hawaii. If traveling solo, mutter to yourself.

SAMPLE TEST SUMMARY

Our sample vacationers happen to be a newly married, outdoor-oriented couple. Their chosen "Gotta-Have-It" categories (refer to Best Of category numbers) are good snorkeling, and wild, quiet beaches to hike and spend the day. They also want attractions and visitors centers, botanical gardens, rain forests, and bird-watching forests. They also want to mountain bike.

Our couple's "Would-be-nice" choices are for coastal-bluff trails, whale watching, watching surfers, checking out museums and galleries, and visiting Hawaiian temples, and tourist towns.

After referring to the Best Of Scorecard on page 66, our couple notes that Kaua'i wins 6 of their 9 Gotta-Have-It categories. Kaua'i is the clear winner! Just to be thorough, they read the results for category 29 (rain forests), and note that Kaua'i finishes second. For category 2 (overall snorkeling), our couple notes that Kaua'i has three listings in the top 20, including a boldfaced listing (Tunnels).

For the other category that Kaua'i did not win, (19-Attractions & Visitors Centers), Kaua'i has four top-20 listings, and also a boldfaced attraction (Kilauea Wildlife Refuge).

SELF-TEST SAMPLE RESULTS

GOTTA-HAVE-IT		WOULD-BE-NICE	
Cat. #	Island	Cat. #	Island
2	M	7	BI
5	K	10	M
8	K	15	O
9	K	18	O
19	O	20	BI
21	K	22	O
29	BI		
32	K		
34	K/BI (tie)		

KEY:
Numbers refer to Best Of categories.

K = Kauai
O = Oahu
M = Maui
BI = Big Island

Among the Would-Be-Nice listings, Kaua'i does poorly. However, when our couple refers to the results for each category, they see that Kaua'i does have entries, so these shortcomings aren't enough to affect their decision.

BEST OF CATEGORIES Use for self-test. See Scorecard on page 66 for winners.

Swimming & Snorkeling Beaches

1. BEGINNER SNORKELING
Easiest-entry, fish-filled calm waters to get you hooked on snorkeling.

2. OVERALL GOOD SNORKELING
Best spots for snorkelers with experience.

3. QUEENS BATHS, FRESH POOLS & KEIKI (KID) BEACHES
Queens baths (tide pools) make great pools, when surf is low. Slack rivers provide freshwater swimming opportunities. Reefs near shore form pools, with calm, shallow waters perfect for toddlers and dawdlers.

4. FAMILY DAY AT THE BEACH
Jump in the car with the kids and beach gear and spread out for a day of fun in the surf, sand, and sun.

5. A BOOK, A BEACH, AND THEE
Couples can find a shaded nook at the edge of the sand and spend a quiet day, taking dips to cool off, joined by few other beachgoers—at undeveloped beaches.

6. BABE & HUNK BEACHES
Check out the be-seen scene and stake out some sand of your own.

Coastal Hiking & Beachcombing

7. COASTAL BLUFFS, TIDE POOLS, BIG WAVES CRASH
Trails in the salt spray of dramatic seascapes and spots to watch explosions of white water.

8. HIKE-TO WILD BEACHES
Unspoiled beaches only reachable by foot from inshore trailhead parking.

9. DRIVE-UP WILD AND SCENIC BEACHES
Park at the beach and then go barefoot or use surf shoes along a mile or more of an unspoiled beach.

10. WHALES & WILDLIFE
During winter and early spring, you can see migrating humpbacks offshore just about anywhere. But where are the best places? Dolphins, big sea turtles, and Hawaii's endangered monk seals also draw admirers. Seabirds are a coastal alternative for birdwatchers.

Surfing & Wind-wave Sports

11. WAVES FOR THE BIG BOYS
Pros come from around the globe to test their skills.

12. RELIABLE SPOTS FOR GOOD SURFERS
Usually waves, big or small, depending on the day.

13. LEARN-TO-SURF BEACHES
Instructors can get you up to ride the near-shore surf.

14. BODYBOARDING
Belly on the board, rolling in the white water.

15. BEST PLACES TO WATCH SURFERS
It's a free-flowing spectator sport that can be addictive. Watch from all angles.

16. WINDSURFING & KITE-BOARDING
Harnessing the wind, lots of colorful sails flitting around behind and over the waves. It's a kick just to watch.

17. KAYAKING RIVERS & OCEAN
No whitewater here. Head up jungle rivers and lagoons—and possibly hike to a waterfall. Paddle remote coastlines, reef-protected bays, and to islands close to shore.

Sightseeing & Entertainment

18. MUSEUMS & GALLERIES
Some of the best in the world, and many sure to entertain, aloha-style.

19. ATTRACTIONS & VISITORS CENTERS
Aquariums, national parks, sugar cane plantations, Hawaiian cowboys, volcanoes, tsunamis, astronomy, coffee, marine mammals ...

20. HAWAIAN TEMPLES AND ANCIENT SITES
Explore the remnants of the Polynesian civilization that came from the South Pacific, beginning in about 100 AD—petroglyphs, shrines, and temples.

21. BOTANICAL GARDENS & ARBORETUMS
Many acres of flowering shrubs and trees—somebody's brainchild. Some of the best in the world.

22. WALK-AROUND TOURIST TOWNS
Shave ice, tee-shirts, cuisine, cocktails, art, antiques, trinkets, historic sites, beachwear, and people watching. Shop, dine, browse, hangout.

23. SWANK RESORTS
Architecture, galleries, décor, fine dining, shops, and poolside gardenscapes. Hawaii has many of the world's best destination resorts and resort strips.

24. INSPIRING CHURCHES & HOLY PLACES
Location, location, location—a wide range of religions have erected dramatic edifices.

25. SCENIC DRIVES
Yes, there are traffic jams in Hawaii, but also many meandering highways worthy of a car commercial

26. PICNIC PARKS
A seaside table awaits in the shade of a swaying palm. Or let birds serenade your table in the forest.

Hikes & Strolls—Mountain & Forest

27. TROPICAL RIDGES & PEAKS
Look down to the sea from those scalloped, towering ridgelines—the emerald escarpments that say "Hawaii."

28. WATERFALLS
Scenic overlooks and longer hikes to where all that rain gathers and drops in white ribbons and cascades.

29. RAIN FOREST & STREAM VALLEYS
An overwhelming profusion of greenery in all directions at arm's length.

30. EASY WALKS TO CLASSIC HAWAIIAN VIEWS
Places where you get a faraway vista (and beat the crowd) not far from the car.

31. DRY AND HIGH
The leeward sides have canyons with cacti and dwarf flora, and many of Hawaii's peaks are above the treeline. You'll be reminded of the American Southwest, only floating in the Pacific Ocean.

32. BIRDWATCHING FORESTS
Twitters and chirps from deep within the forest.

33. VOLCANO CRATERS & LAVA
Technically, all Hawaiian hikes are in this category, but on these you'll know it for sure.

Sports on Land

34. BICYCLE TOURING & MOUNTAIN BIKING
Tour scenic roads and bike paths, or get muddy on dirt coastal or ridge roads.

35. HORSEBACK RIDING
Ride coastal bluffs or verdant, high pastures.

36. GOLF
Lots of choices, several where the pros play.

Waimea Canyon and Waipoo Falls, Kauai

NIIHAU

KAUAI
map page 31

OAHU
map page 32

MOLOKAI

The Islands Of Hawaii

LANAI

MAUI
map page 33

KAHOOLAWE

HAWAII
THE BIG ISLAND
map page 34

WHAT'S YOUR TYPE? PICK THE LOCALE THAT RINGS YOUR CHIMES.

It's time to imagine the locale of your dreams, or at least of your reasonable expectations. You have choices. Paradoxically, you can travel from island to island and stay in the same locale. Or you can stay in wildly varying locales on the same island.

Hawaii's landmass makes it one of the smallest states, but smallness here translates to a broad choice of vacation locales—from ultra-glam resorts, to quaint cottages in small towns, to outright wilderness, all within a hour's drive.

The Big Island, larger than all the other islands combined, has 11 of the earth's 13 possible climatic zones. It is comprised of five separate volcanoes joined together by eruptions that span a million years. Similarly, the north and south sides of Maui are two distinctly different volcanoes now joined by an isthmus. And the Maui of today was in geologic yesteryear a connected landmass—Maui Nui—that included Lanai, Molokai, and Kahalo'owae. On Oahu, you notice two mountain ranges—the Ko'olaus and the Waianaes—that were separate island volcanoes. Kaua'i is similarly formed, though five million years have disguised the geographic clues.

Among all the islands, a typical weather pattern creates an environmental consistency: All the islands have a windward side and leeward side. In the winter, north- and northeast-facing shores, receive the trade winds and more frequent rainfall, and thus sport tropical greenery and fluted, waterfall-laced escarpments. Southern and southwestern shores, the leeward sides, are comparatively arid, home to scrub and cactus. Sunny leeward coasts are the sites of the luxury resorts and beachside communities.

The second typical weather pattern is mauka (mountain) showers. The highest reaches of the islands draw clouds and rain, making them rain forests in many cases. Even on windward shores, mauka heights will get several times the rainfall of the coast. An exception is the Big Island, where the 13,000-plus-foot peaks of Mauna Loa and Mauna Kea are barren and arid, and the mauka-shower effect is seen in the lower band around them. Maui's Haleakala is also arid at the peak.

So, no matter which island you choose, you need to further decide which locale seems right, and affordable. Rub knuckles into your closed eye sockets and envision where you want to spend your time in Hawaii. What do you see? (Picking a specific lodging within a locale is covered in the next section.)

Iao Needle, Maui

LOCALE ONE
SUNNY BEACHFRONT TOURIST TOWNS WITH MID-PRICED CONDOS, RESORTS, RESTAURANTS, AND SHOPPING

KAUA'I
Coconut Coast, between Kapa'a and Wailua —Resorts are nicely spaced along the coast, which was the chosen home of Kaua'i's ancient royalty for its wide river, coral coast, and verdant interior. Eastern exposure is out of the rain belt, but not arid. Coral-reef and small yellow-sand beaches offer snorkeling (in calm weather) and good strolling. Kapa'a and Wailua have both family and fancy restaurants. Some great hiking lies just inland, at Mt. Waialeale and the Sleeping Giant. You're midway between Waimea Canyon and the north shore, making the Coconut Coast convenient for day-trippers.

You may want to avoid: Nawiliwili, the working harbor below Lihue, has a few condos and hotels that are priced right. Although Kalapaki Bay and the posh Marriott are nearby, your accommodations may be in complexes that cater to longer term rentals, so Nawiliwili may be a little humdrum for vacationers.

OAHU
Waikiki—Mixed in with beachfront luxury resorts are high-rise hotels that cater to the more budget-oriented traveler. Waikiki is a city for tourists, a six-block grid between the ocean and Ala Wai Canal that ranges from tacky to tasteful in both its shopping and dining. Many headline attractions are within walking distance. Trolley and shuttle services will get you to Pearl Harbor, Honolulu, and Hanauma Bay snorkeling. Beaches are safe for swimming, though not the most scenic, in spite of the Diamond Head view. A number of Oahu's best hiking trails lie in the mountains above—across densely packed metro Honolulu. Waikiki is blessed with lots of Hawaiian sun.

You may want to avoid: Locals will laugh out loud and think you're brave if you plan to vacation on the West Side, around Waianae. Even visitors familiar with everyplace else in Hawaii will get a jab of culture shock. The coastal towns indeed are rough around the edges, but the West Side, with great heads of land that jut from the Waianae Range and reach the sea at bays and beaches, is one of the most beautiful coasts in Hawaii. And the tough-guy image—to validate a cliché—hides a warm, kind Old-Hawaii community that will be open to visitors who are respectful and friendly.

Locale One, Sunny Beachfront Tourist Towns cont'd —

MAUI

Kihei — The southwest coast of Maui, a.k.a, the Gold Coast, is a run of nice sandy beaches, offering safe swimming at family beach parks. Kihei has a wide selection of condominiums and mid-level resorts, interspersed in a few-miles-long commercial district chockablock with eateries, shops, and prosaic stores. While it lacks historical interest or central charm, Kihei has all the elements to deliver a good vacation. Sun shines on Kihei, winter and summer, though don't sue someone if it rains. Traffic gets bottled up trying to get through the center of the island to destinations like Haleakala and the Hana Highway. Most accommodations are across a street from the beach; avoid places that are blocks inland.

Lahaina— Once the capital of the islands under King Kamehameha, and later the site of the whaling and missionary movements, Lahaina is a fascinating tourist town. And it's set in a boat harbor offering offshore adventures, as well a ferries to Lanai and Molokai. Good beaches flank the commercial zone. Jade green mountains rise inland. Lahaina has several mid-range resorts and condos, although most of that is farther north on the highway, and much of the backstreets are modest-sized homes and cottages. Maui's nightlife is centered here, and the place is usually humming with tourists during the day. Lahaina is just south of the rain belt, so sun is the rule.

Honokowai-Kahana-Kapalua— The several miles of beaches and bays north of ritzy Ka'anapali, once the domain of powerful King Pi'ilani, now might be dubbed the Condo Coast. Some of Maui's smaller, kitschy resorts are densely packed at the shoreline, alongside condominium complexes and higher-end timeshares. The newer highway bypasses this zone (you wouldn't call it a town). Napili Bay offers excellent beachgoing, as does Kapalua Bay. Offshore views of Molokai and Lanai add charm. Traffic in and out is not fun, but families can squirrel away in their newfound nooks. Prices will go up as you go north, with Honokowai in the south and Kapalua in the north.

Ma'alaea— Located in the middle of the bay on the west side of the isthmus that separates north and south Maui, Ma'alaea is an easier getaway than either Kihei or the Lahaina. You can get better prices at these high rises. The beach is better for walking and jogging than swimming. People don't flock here, but some visitors may like the more out-of-the-way feel. It can be windy.

You may want to avoid: Kahului, near the airport, is on the working end bay, opposite the isthmus from Ma'alaea. A few hotels offer moderate prices. These beachfronts are more of a base of operations than a place to spend the day. The non-tourist neighborhood may appeal to independent travelers. Wailuku is the county seat adjacent to Kahului. You won't find beachfront, but you can find a value in a non-tourist area that will appeal to visitors who want to keep it real.

BIG ISLAND

Kailua-Kona —Kailua (or Kona as it is known) is a tourist town with historical roots, similar to Maui's Lahaina. This is where the big guy, Kamehameha I, chose to live the last decade of his life. A range of restaurants and tourist shops line the main drag, Ali'i Drive, and a few blocks inland are actual shopping centers. Cruise ships deliver throngs of visitors to the mix. A few hotels, including the Kamehameha Resort, are in the historic district at the harbor in the north. The southern end of the 3-mile coast features more condominiums. Keahou, on the south end of Kailua, has some good, quieter condos, as well as the newly opened Keahou Sheraton—Kona's finest resort. Some Kona condos are beachfront, but most are across Ali'i Drive. Most people are surprised to learn Kona lacks a long sandy beach, but a few smaller beaches offer very good snorkeling and swimming. Kealakekua Bay and the beaches of South Kona are easy reaches for day trips. The farthest south in the islands, Kona can be counted on for sun, although all that Kona coffee just up the mountain does see its share of rain. Vog—volcanic smog—is Kona's dirty secret, and some days it can be quite hazy. Traffic for several miles either side of Kona is often gridlocked.

Hilo Bay — Let's be clear: 'sunny' and 'Hilo' are not often used in the same sentence. But several high-rise hotels stand at the shore of the bay, next to Liliuokalani Gardens and picturesque Coconut Island (Moku Ola). A range of restaurants, many priced for working families, is nearby though not walking distance. Hilo's legendary rains, and lack of a long sand beach, make Hilo Bay a second-tier option, but several of these hotels have been renovated and more moderate pricing make them a smart choice. The view across the bay is one of the best in Hawaii, and the gardens are an excellent walk. Unheralded beach parks nearby offer excellent swimming—in good weather.

LOCALE TWO
HIGHER END BEACHFRONT RESORT STRIPS

KAUA'I
Poipu Beach — Year-around sunshine and a run of safe, family beaches have brought high-end condos set in pleasant green spaces, as well as the comfortably fancy Sheraton Kaua'i. In nearby Prince Kuhio are less-expensive condos and a few beach cottages, near one of the island's best snorkeling coves. The arid climate and gently sloping backshore don't shout "Hawaii," but just south of Poipu is the wild coastline of Mahaulepu, set below dramatic Hoary Head Ridge—a quick getaway for hikers, cyclists, and equestrians. Koloa Town is just up the hill, offering a folksier dining alternative to Poipu's more glamorous, resort-development options. An easy getaway to Waimea Canyon, but the north shore is a full day trip.

Princeville — It's hard to pigeonhole Princeville. Sitting upon a green bluff above Hanalei Bay are the world-class Princeville Hotel, the nice Hanalei Bay Resort, and scads of high- to middle-range condominiums and rental homes, situated around golf courses. Some of the newer units are crammed together. The lower-priced condos are longer-term rentals, with accompanying neighborhood noise. Overall Princeville is tasteful, and features four or five beaches you can walk down to and several hiking trails inland. A shopping center is nearby for practical needs. The immediate surroundings are ranchlands and estate homes on large parcels. Hanalei Bay is a few miles away. With the north shore's beauty come winter rains.

Princeville Resort, Kauai

Locale Two, Higher End Beachfront Resort Strips cont'd —

OAHU

Waikiki — Hawaiian tourism was invented here, at two venerable resorts, the Royal Hawaiian and Moana Surfrider, which still feel like Old Hawaii, though literally encased by the towers of glittering Waikiki. Several other deluxe options are available, including the Hilton Hawaiian Village and the artful Halekulani Resort. Waikiki is the Vegas of the Pacific. Waikiki will be like you imagine it to be, yet much of it defies imagination. Major attractions are within walking distance or nearby (Diamond Head, Hanauma Bay, Honolulu, Pearl Harbor). Honolulu's museums and sites are a short trolley ride away.

Ko Olina — A realization of a developer's fantasy across a harbor from slag heaps, Ko Olina delivers a high-quality Hawaii resort experience, set apart from Waikiki on the sunny West Side. A series of man-made coves create excellent swimming opportunities. A new ultra-shopping mall is in the works, which will feature a swim-with-the-dolphins pool. Condos and town homes fringe a golf course at the backshore, while the signature resort (home to NFL's pro-bowlers) and new high-rise beach clubs lord over the lagoons.

MAUI

Ka'anapali — Set just north of Lahaina, Ka'anapali features the all-stars of luxury resorts—Grand Hyatt, Marriott, Westin, and Sheraton—connected by a poolside garden path that is the gateway to several beaches. It the 70's, Sheraton's run of sand was called Dig Me Beach. You dig? Swimming, snorkeling, surfing are all good-to-excellent. Opulent shopping opportunities can be had at the Whaler's Village, hardly a village. A few high-end resorts stand alone, in view of the Ka'anapali strip, including the Royal Lahaina. The tourist commute creates gridlock.

Wailea — Four destination resorts stand shoulder-to-shoulder on the sunny coast just south of Kihei, several of which make it to the world's-best lists in well known travel magazines (Fairmont Kea Lani, Four Seasons, Grand Wailea, and Renaissance Wailea Beach). A nearly two-mile walking path fronts the resorts, providing entrée to several inviting pockets of white sand beaches and ending at long Keawakapu Beach. The resorts' gardenscapes are isolated from their neighbors, no doubt a security-oriented move, and only an on-street sidewalk connects the establishments inland of the beach. Of course, gourmet restaurants and luxury shopping are sprinkled about, and several golf courses buffet the arid hills above. Wailea offers its well-heeled guests and conventioneers an impeccable, pampered resort experience.

BIG ISLAND
Doesn't have a comparable locale

LOCALE THREE
BEACH DESTINATION RESORTS

Quite a few of the world's top-rated luxury resorts are in Hawaii. This is where the Big Island shines. You will pay top dollar, of course. At these places and prices, visitors will spend a lot of time hanging around the opulent resort grounds. See *Best Of*, page 108.

Wailea, Maui

LOCALE FOUR
BEACH COTTAGES IN RURAL OR NEIGHBORHOOD SETTINGS

KAUA'I

Hanalei — When the waterfalls adorn cliffs of Waioli Valley and the frothy blue surf is roll-ing into the bay, Hanalei meets just about everyone's fantasy of what a tropical beach town should be. Cottages and homes are set in a quiet, ten-by-five block grid, all within walking distance of town. Two shopping areas are off street, in funky malls, and other boutiques and adventure outfitters occupy the woodframes at the outskirts of the town. You may get big surf and rain in the winter. When surf is flat in the summer, the aquamarine coastline is habit-forming, and such a sweet place as this can only be criticized for being too popular.

Anini Beach —A long coral reef creates a mild shoreline, with beachfront homes and cottages nicely spaced along a two-mile, dead-end lane. Anini is a getaway beach, perfect for a Big Chill weekend among friends or a family reunion. The beach park has good snorkeling, kayak-ing, and windsurfing. A polo field hosts a summer league. Anini is north shore, but not as far out as Hanalei or even Princeville, making it easier to base there and take day trips elsewhere. There are no shops or restaurants.

You may want to avoid: Kapa'a's beachside cottage offerings are sprinkled into the working neighborhood, often viewless and noisy. But Kapa'a does have a big upside for visitors: The younger hemp-set gathers for vegan wraps and chai tea. Open-air bars waft boozy conserva-tion into the night air. A coastal path leads to several, small coral beaches and cyclists can go for miles. Good hiking lies inland. Find the right spot and you'll feel at home in Kapa'a.

Your may want to avoid: Kekaha and Waimea, on the west side, are fun to visit, but too far out and too neighborhoody for the average visitor. Kekaha's sunny, long sand beach has high surf and no shade; Waimea Bay's water is often murky due to river runoff. Exception: Waimea Plantation Cottages are well kept and quaint, situated on an expanse of greenery.

OAHU

Lanikai-Kailua — Lanikai is a one of Oahu's glamour-puss beaches. Often the setting for com-mercials and catalogue shoots, the neighborhood of beach cottages lies between stand-alone Kawai Ridge and Lanikai Beach. Most of Lanikai is set back from the beach, which is acces-sible via a series of short paths. Some visitors may prefer Kailua's less popular beach cottages, set on the opposite side of the town and Kailua Beach Park. The Kailua options are less cloistered, stretched along Kalama Beach, over a mile long. The Kailua cottage area gives way to ritzy, gated homes, and then to the verboten Kaneohe Marine Corps Base. This wind-ward locale is densely populated and Kailua itself is surprisingly drab, though it has a number of good eateries and watering holes.

Waimanalo — Between a beach park and a large state recreation area is a ten-block neigh-borhood of beach homes with a number of access points to a beautiful beach. The Ko'olau Mountains rise dramatically inland and Rabbit Island adds to the seascape. Prices will be down from Lanikai-Kailua. Waimanalo is more home to native Hawaiians than tourists and many of Hawaii's slack-key guitar greats call these shores home.

North Shore — Banzai Pipeline, Sunset Beach, Waimea Bay—the stuff songs and surfer mov-ies are made of. But don't expect glitz on Oahu's North Shore. In and above Haleiwa, the main

Locale Four, Beach Cottages in Rural or Neighborhood Settings cont'd —

town, are small B&B-type rentals and owner-owned cottages. You can get an outer-island experience on the laid back North Shore. A bike lane covers much of the distance and there are plenty of beaches, in addition to the famous ones. The inland area of this shore rises to modest heights and does not carry the photo-quality punch of other Oahu locales.

You might want to avoid: Get too far from the coast on Oahu or away from the areas mentioned above and you may have a suburban experience.

MAUI

Hana—For all the falderal of the Hana Highway, you won't find many tourist accommodations in Hana. But score yourself a cottage in the community and a whole new outdoor world will open up, in the mountains and on the coast, that you don't have time for when making the day trip. Don't expect a lot of "action." Hana is rural, offering a few good beaches along a rugged coastline.

Paia — Surfers, vegans, and the island's gentry roam the shops and restaurants of the three or four blocks of the T-intersection at Paia. Cars usually form a conga line through town, making strolls less carefree. Windsurfing capital Ho'okipia Beach is a couple miles away, as is beautiful Baldwin Beach Park, but the beaches right in town aren't great. Private rentals are tucked away, both in town and up Baldwin Avenue, which leads to the upcountry. The best beach cottages are to be had a couple miles toward Kahului, in Spreckelsville, near the Maui Country Club.

Lahaina — A number of cottage rentals are mixed into the fringes of Lahaina, which is listed in Locale One above. The south end of town on the ocean side of the highway is preferable.

BIG ISLAND

Puako — Most of the Big Island's best beaches are hidden in oases along the 25 miles of sun-scorched lava of South Kohala, and all of these beaches are either parklands with no accommodations or at destination resorts. The exception is Puako. Along a 3-mile dead-end coastal road are cottages, homes, and new estates. The shoreline is all reef, one favored by sea turtles and migrating whales. A short path leads from one end of Puako to the sprawling, lovely grounds of the Fairmont Orchid and Mauna Lani. Going the other way via a bumpy road is Hapuna Beach State Park and the Mauna Kea Hotel.

Kanaha Beach Park, Maui

Kealakekua — A five-mile road descends to the bay, a snorkeling haven and home to Pu'uhonua o Honaunau National Park. It's a bit of a drive to get up the hill and into Kona, or anywhere else, but the owner-owned rentals in Kealakekua are a true getaway. A state monument features the heiau that first welcomed the ships of Captain Cook—and later became his last anchorage. A nearby Ke'ei Village is about as far off the beaten path as you can get on the coast.

The Puna Coast — East Hawaii is a beautiful tropical drive and you will find some amazing tide-pool snorkeling and geothermal pools for dipping. But the place will be a little out-there (both literally and figuratively) for most visitors.

LOCALE FIVE
INNS , CONDOS, AND COTTAGES IN PASTORAL OR MOUNTAIN SETTINGS

KAUAʻI
Kilauea — Between the Coconut Coast and Hanalei, pasturelands and small farms extend upward from the coast toward the fissured ridges of interior Kauaʻi. Guest homes and cottages make for ideal getaways for independent travelers. Several hike-to beaches and the Kilauea Point National Wildlife Refuge are all-star attractions nearby. **You may want to avoid:** The town of Kilauea is a neighborhood grid of homes, some of which have guest accommodations with no views that may not feel like a vacation.

Wailua Homesteads — This is a rural zone between the Sleeping Giant (mountain) above Kapaʻa and the interior ridges that include the famous Mt. Waialeale. You can find cottages often on the grounds of larger homes in quiet country settings with acreage. Great local hiking options, and the beaches of Coconut Coast are nearby. Central location makes this a good choice for touring other destinations. **You may want to avoid:** Some of the cottages (ohana houses) may be packed into someone's back yard in a neighborhood, giving you remoteness without the privacy. This can be particularly true in Kapahi—up Kawaihau Road on the Kealia end of Kapaʻa.

Omao and Lawai valleys, Kalaheo — These communities are in the semi-rural upslopes above the sunny shores of Poipu. Not many tourist accommodations, but you can find a country cottage within neighborhoods. **You may want to avoid:** Ask the right questions to make sure you're not pigeonholed into a neighborhood that won't feel like a vacation.

Koloa — Cutesy, old-timey Koloa is a couple miles up the hill from Poipu Beach. You can find good views and privacy, but also houses tucked into the flat, in a more closely packed residential area. Koloa offers quick getaways to west Kauaʻi and Waimea Canyon, and not a bad day trip to the north shore.

OAHU
Oahu is weak in this category. The steep mountain ranges (Waianaes and Koʻolaus) are watersheds with no development, and suburban development is tucked up to their bases. Your best chance to be in trees with birds is the North Shore, at rentals above Pupukea.

MAUI
Makawao and Haiku — Above the ocean on the east side at Paia, and well down the big mountain of Haleakala, is a treed greenbelt with plenty of room for cottages and ohana houses on larger estates. Makawao has character in its shops and restaurants. Some of Maui's low-key Hollywood types and socialites are squirreled away in these hills. You'll often get views, quietude, and privacy at a decent price. There's good access to Haleakala, windward coast, and Hana Highway, and not bad to get across to Kihei and Lahaina, since you're going opposite the tourist commute. Windward exposure means less sun.

Kula — Maui's true upcountry lies along the contour highway about 4,000 feet up on Haleakala's north face. There a few quirky shops and restaurants, but not a town of Kula per se. Good access to Haleakala and the trails of Poli Poli Springs State Park, but a long doubleback to drive down to beaches. A few cottages and rental homes are available. And bring a nice warm top, since it's chilly up there. You can get great views across to the West Maui Mountains, and you'll feel delightfully isolated from the tourist hubbub.

Locale Five, Inns, Condos and Cottages in Pastoral or Mountain Settings cont'd —

You may want to avoid—Huelo is at the north end of the Hana Highway, on a bluff on the ocean side of the highway. A few cottages and guest accommodations will have blue water views, set in dense gardenscapes. Easy access to the Hana Highway and Paia; a long haul to everyplace else. You can get a sense of exclusivity, tucked about the warm and wild seascape—but not exactly at a competitive price.

BIG ISLAND

Volcano — Just a mile from the main entrance to Hawaii Volcanoes National Park, Volcano is a spread-around village set in native ohia-and-tree-fern rain forest at a cool 4,000 feet in elevation. Aside from the tasteful Kilauea Inn, most accommodations are B&Bs and by-owner rental cottages. The locale is perfect for visiting the national park, especially during the morning and evening hours when many tourists must flee. It's also an easy shot down the mountain to see Hilo and the Puna Coast. South Point and Black Sand Beach are an easy day trip the other direction down the mountain. Though you'll need outerwear, the birdland forests of Volcano are, yes, enchanting.

Honoka'a-Waipio-Hamakua Coast-Pepe'ekeo — The highway north of Hilo winds through the tropical greenery that people expect from Hawaii. Pepe'ekeo is just north of Hilo, on the southern end of 40 miles of scenic highway to Honoka'a, which is close to Waipio Valley. The road is high above the coast with no beaches except a couple of rugged beach parks, but it offers hiking trails at Kalopa State Park and Akaka Falls State Park. You'll find cottages and rentals in and around old sugar towns and local neighborhoods. Prices are right, normally. From Hamakua Coast, Waipio Valley is an easy day trip, as is Hilo. The Puna Coast and Hawaii Volcanoes National Park are very doable as day trips, as are Mauna Kea and Mauna Loa.

Hawi-Kapa'au — The green nubbin of Kohala is closer to Maui in both geologic age and distance than it is to South Point on the Big Island. These two sugar towns are Old Hawaii, with welcoming sense of community and some subtle big money mixed into its forested highlands. By-owner cottages and a few Euro-style inns will interest independent travelers. It may seem far from everything, but the fantastic hike into Pololu Valley is at road's end, historic sites and good snorkeling spots are just down the road, and the beaches of South Kohala are a scenic, easy day trip. The towns offer galleries, local art ware, and some good restaurant choices—all spread along a rural highway that goes from pleasantly pastoral to dramatically tropical.

Kona Mauka —A few B&Bs, inns, and by-owner cottages are located well above the coast, beginning north of Kailua at the airport and extending for some 15 miles to the south. Rentals will refer to various communities, which, listed north to south, are Kona-Mauka, Kailua-Kona, Holualoa, Keahou, Kainilau, Kealakekua, Captain Cook, and Honaunau. **You may want to avoid:** You need to pick and choose, and ask the right questions to avoid getting sandwiched into a neighborhood setting. Upper Keahou is good, as is the high ground above Kealakekua Bay at Captain Cook and Honaunau. Touristy Kona is readily accessible, as are the beaches of South Kohala and Kealakekua. Traffic in and out of Kona has become more than a nuisance.

Wood Valley-Pahala-Na'alehu — As you drive from South Point toward Hawaii Volcanoes National Park, a world of greenery opens up inland—the Kau Forest Reserve and the newest addition to the national park. Pahala has sugar-shacks in a neighborhood setting. Na'alehu is more of a town, with a few good eateries, and the nearby Sea Mountain Resort, the only sort-of-fancy place around—nice condos on a golf course. Wood Valley is a few miles up the road, entirely rural. If you seek off-the-tourist-track but still very scenic, check it out. Black Sand Beach, with hidden Hawaiian ancient sites, is nearby, as is South Point and Green Sand Beach. You can also jog up the South Kona coast to Miloli'i, but everything else on the Big Island is not a practical day trip from these locales.

You may want to avoid: Waimea-Kamulea is the main town of the huge Parker Ranch, along a scenic drive of rolling pasturelands beneath towering Mauna Kea and the Kohala Mountains. It's only when you stop that some shortcomings are apparent: there are no parks or trails, since access is tied up by the ranch and Hawaiian Homelands. The town itself, though featuring several top-end restaurants, lacks a central charm and offers instead a standard strip mall. Weather can often be chilly, and traffic gets snarled. With all that, many people will like Waimea as a stopover, and you'll find tasteful cottages and several reputable inns, as well as a smattering of galleries and giftstores.

You may want to avoid Waikaloa Village — Many "villages" really aren't, and Waikaloa is no exception. Set inland about 15 miles on the volcanic slopes and mid-distance along the South Kohala Coast, Waikaloa Village is an assemblage of condominium complexes built around a golf course and shopping center. You can find some deluxe units, but prices aren't "economy," and some of the offerings are more working neighborhoods than vacation destinations. A nearby neighborhood has homes with views.

You may want to avoid: Pahoa, Kurtistown, and Mountain View lie in the rain forest between Hilo and the national park. Since this a large area and in a high-risk zone for Mauna Loa eruptions, property values are low. You'll find non-conforming rentals and "hideaways" that may be too wild-and-wooly for tourists. Rainfall can also be incessant.

You might really want to avoid: On the Kona side of South Point is Ocean View, a community of homes built upon a hellishly vast slag heap of a'a (sharp) lava. Many nice people live here and they are happy, no doubt, but this place has little appeal to visitors.

Waimea Plantation Cottages, Big Island

STRATEGIES FOR VISITING YOUR ISLAND

Will you be able to easily see all you want to see from the locale of your dreams? The short answer is yes, except for the Big Island, where switching locales makes the most sense. But even on the smaller islands, you may want to hop around.

KAUA'I

Everyplace is reachable by car in one day, so where you stay is a matter of personal taste. To stay centrally with the easiest day-trip option, try the Coconut Coast. To split your time, stay about one-third time in Poipu and the rest on the northern shores (Princeville, Kilauea, Hanalei, or Haena).

OAHU

You can get anywhere in Oahu in one day from anywhere else. Some of those days will be long. Most Oahu visitors stay in Waikiki and branch out from there to nearby Honolulu, Pearl Harbor, and Hanauma Bay. You don't really need a rental car to stay in Waikiki, which saves money.

For a lower key Oahu, stay on the North Shore, or on the Windward Coast in Kailua-Lanikai, and venture into Waikiki to check it out. For the yin yang, alternate accommodations between the North Shore and Waikiki.

MAUI

All the sights of Maui are within a day's drive. Almost all tourists stay on the west side, either in south in Kihei-Wailea or on the north end at Lahaina-Ka'anapali-Kapalua. As an alternative, try a few days in low-key Hana, where most people drive through in the midday tourist train and don't have time to appreciate this lush side of Maui. Makawao-Haiku will also appeal to visitors who want out of the main tourist zones.

Another option on Maui is to visit Lanai or Molokai, both of which lie an hour's ferry ride west from Lahaina. Lanai, a privately held island first owned by Dole, now has two luxury hotels and the more rustic hotel in Lanai City, a sleepy former pineapple town. Molokai, by contrast, is where locals rule, and a number of low-key resorts and condo complexes are scattered about

the island. Lanai makes an easier day trip, as you can ride hotel shuttle buses and hit the local highlights. You'll want a car and at least an overnight to see Molokai.

BIG ISLAND

On one long, scenic day trip, it is possible to get anywhere on the Big Island and then return to your digs, although in some cases you'll have little time for activities along the way. If you're staying two weeks or longer, consider two or three locales.

The traditional two-locale option is Hilo-Kona, which are 100 miles apart, whichever way you choose to drive the circle. From Hilo you see Waipio Valley, Puna, and Hawaii Volcanoes National Park. From Kona, you can day trip to Kohala, South Kohala Beaches, Kealakekua, and South Point. Mauna Loa and Mauna Kea—two of Hawaii's memorable adventures—can be visited from either locale.

But you don't need to stay around Kona at all, and, although you'll be away from the concentration of shopping and restaurants, you will also avoid traffic. There are different ways to stay on opposite sides of the island. Hamakua-Na'alehu is an offbeat one. Hawi-Volcano is also a non-traditional option that works. Or, triangulate with, say, Hawi-Hilo-Wood Valley; or perhaps divide your stay among Waimea-Volcano-Kealakekua.

TIME TO MOVE ON

Alright, you've picked an island, have a bead on what you want to do, and know what kind of locale sounds best. You have in mind the kind of vacation you'd like and what you want out of it. Time to do Da Plan, which begins in the next section.

Makapuu Beach Park, Oahu; Makalawai Oasis, Big Island; Mahaulepu cliff, Kauai; Waialeale Blue Hole waterfalls, Kauai

Pololu Valley Overlook, Big Island; Lahaina hula, Maui; Makaha canoe, Big Island; Princeville Ranch, Kauai

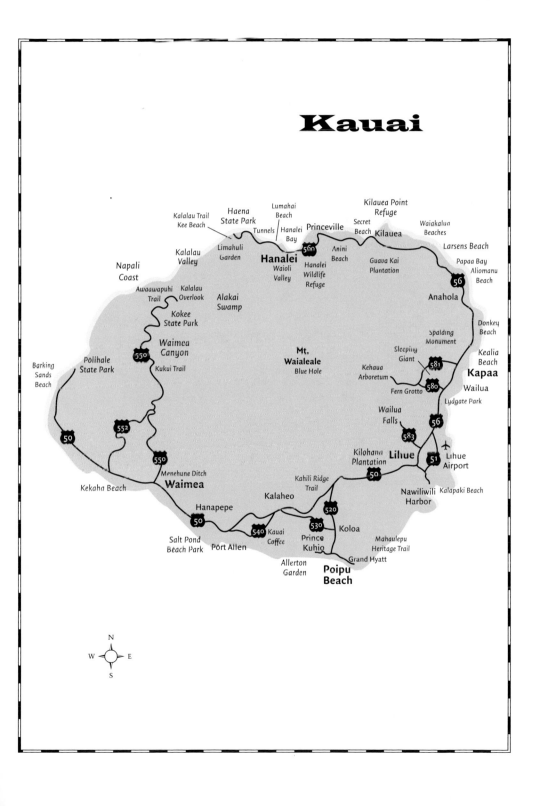

Kauai

Napali Coast

Kalalau Trail
Kee Beach

Haena State Park

Tunnels

Lumahai Beach

Hanalei Bay

Princeville

Kilauea Point Refuge

Secret Beach

Kilauea

Waiakalua Beaches

Larsens Beach

Kalalau Valley

Limahuli Garden

Hanalei

Waioli Valley

Anini Beach

Hanalei Wildlife Refuge

Guava Kai Plantation

560

Papaa Bay

Aliomanu Beach

56

Awaawapuhi Trail

Kalalau Overlook

Alakai Swamp

Anahola

Kokee State Park

Waimea Canyon

Kukui Trail

Mt. Waialeale

Blue Hole

Spalding Monument

Sleeping Giant

Kehaua Arboretum

Donkey Beach

Kealia Beach

Kapaa

581

Barking Sands Beach

Polihale State Park

550

Fern Grotto

580

Wailua

Lydgate Park

552

Wailua Falls

583

56

50

550

Menehune Ditch

Waimea

Kilohana Plantation

Lihue

51

Lihue Airport

Kekaha Beach

Kahili Ridge Trail

50

Kalaheo

Nawiliwili Harbor

Kalapaki Beach

Hanapepe

520

50

540

Kauai Coffee

530

Prince Kuhio

Koloa

Mahaulepu Heritage Trail

Salt Pond Beach Park

Port Allen

Allerton Garden

Grand Hyatt

Poipu Beach

N
W   E
S

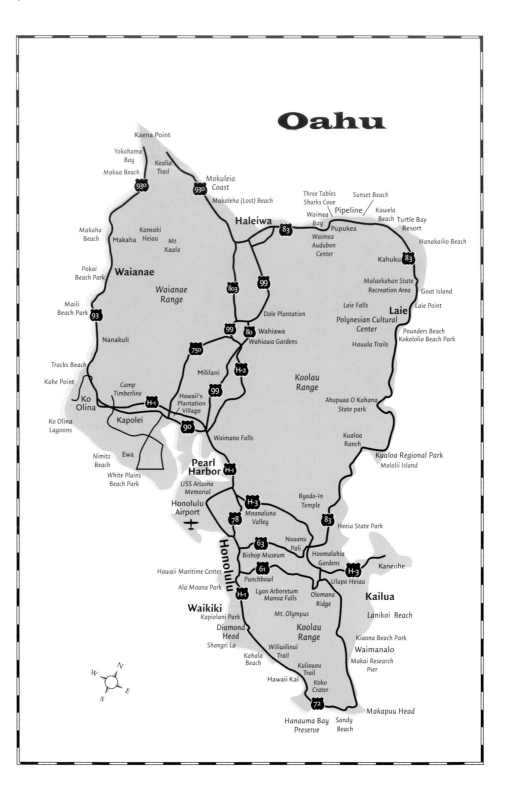

Oahu

Kaena Point

Yokohama Bay
Makua Beach

Kealia Trail

Mokuleia Coast

930

930

Makaleha (Lost) Beach

Three Tables
Sharks Cove

Sunset Beach

Haleiwa

83

Waimea Bay

Pipeline

Kawela Beach

Turtle Bay Resort

Pupukea

Hanakailio Beach

Makaha Beach

Kaneaki Heiau

Makaha

Mt Kaala

Waimea Audubon Center

Kahuku

83

Waianae

Pokai Beach Park

803

99

Malaekahan State Recreation Area

Goat Island

Waianae Range

Laie Falls

Laie

Laie Point

Maili Beach Park

93

99

Dole Plantation

Polynesian Cultural Center

Pounders Beach
Kokololio Beach Park

Nanakuli

750

99

80

Wahiawa

Wahiawa Gardens

Hauula Trails

Tracks Beach

Mililani

H-2

Koolau Range

Kahe Point

Camp Timberline

99

Ko Olina

H-1

Hawaii's Plantation Village

Ahupaa O Kahana State park

Kapolei

90

Ko Olina Lagoons

Waimano Falls

Kualoa Ranch

Nimitz Beach

Ewa

Kualoa Regional Park
Mololii Island

White Plains Beach Park

Pearl Harbor

H-1

USS Arizona Memorial

Byodo-In Temple

Honolulu Airport

H-3

83

Heeia State Park

78

Moanaluna Valley

Honolulu

63

Nuuanu Pali

Bishop Museum

Hoomaluhia Gardens

Kaneohe

Hawaii Maritime Center

61

Punchbowl

Ulupo Heiau

H-3

Ala Moana Park

Lyon Arboretum
Manoa Falls

H-1

Kailua

Waikiki

Olomana Ridge

Lanikai Beach

Kapiolani Park

Diamond Head

Mt. Olympus

Shangri La

Wiliwilinui Trail

Koolau Range

Kiaona Beach Park

Kahala Beach

Kuliouou Trail

Waimanalo

Makai Research Pier

Hawaii Kai

Koko Crater

72

Makapuu Head

Hanauma Bay Preserve

Sandy Beach

N
W   E
S

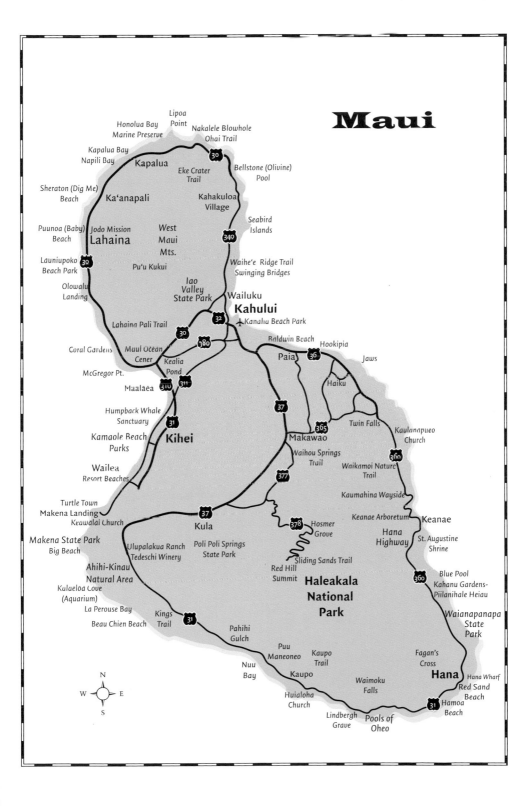

Maui

Lipoa Point
Honolua Bay Marine Preserve
Nakalele Blowhole
Ohai Trail
Kapalua Bay
Napili Bay
Kapalua
Eke Crater Trail
Bellstone (Olivine) Pool
Sheraton (Dig Me) Beach
Ka'anapali
Kahakuloa Village
Seabird Islands
Puunoa (Baby) Beach
Jodo Mission
West Maui Mts.
Lahaina
Launiupoko Beach Park
Pu'u Kukui
Waihe'e Ridge Trail
Swinging Bridges
Olowalu Landing
Iao Valley State Park
Wailuku
Kahului
Lahaina Pali Trail
Kanaha Beach Park
Coral Gardens
Maui Ocean Cener
Kealia Pond
Baldwin Beach
Hookipia
Paia
Jaws
McGregor Pt.
Haiku
Maalaea
Humpback Whale Sanctuary
Kamaole Beach Parks
Kihei
Makawao
Twin Falls
Kaulanapueo Church
Waihou Springs Trail
Waikamoi Nature Trail
Wailea Resort Beaches
Kaumahina Wayside
Turtle Town
Makena Landing
Keawalai Church
Kula
Keanae Arboretum
Keanae
Hosmer Grove
Hana Highway
St. Augustine Shrine
Makena State Park
Big Beach
Ulupalakua Ranch
Tedeschi Winery
Poli Poli Springs State Park
Sliding Sands Trail
Red Hill Summit
Haleakala National Park
Blue Pool
Kahanu Gardens-Piilanihale Heiau
Ahihi-Kinau Natural Area
Kulaeloa Cove (Aquarium)
La Perouse Bay
Kings Trail
Beau Chien Beach
Pahihi Gulch
Waianapanapa State Park
Puu Maneoneo
Kaupo Trail
Fagan's Cross
Nuu Bay
Kaupo
Waimoku Falls
Hana
Hana Wharf
Red Sand Beach
Huialoha Church
Hamoa Beach
Lindbergh Grave
Pools of Oheo

N
W   E
S

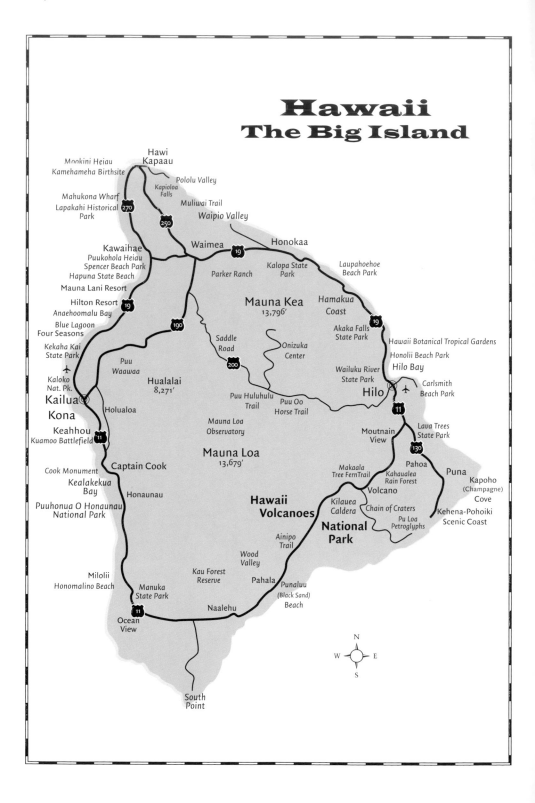

Hawaii
The Big Island

Mookini Heiau
Kamehameha Birthsite

Hawi
Kapaau

Pololu Valley

Kapioloa
Falls

Mahukona Wharf
Lapakahi Historical
Park

270

250

Muliwai Trail

Waipio Valley

Kawaihae
Puukohola Heiau
Spencer Beach Park
Hapuna State Beach

Waimea

19

Honokaa

Mauna Lani Resort

Parker Ranch

Kalopa State
Park

Laupahoehoe
Beach Park

Hilton Resort
Anaehoomalu Bay
Blue Lagoon
Four Seasons

19

Mauna Kea
13,796'

Hamakua
Coast

190

Akaka Falls
State Park

19

Kekaha Kai
State Park

Saddle
Road

Onizuka
Center

Hawaii Botanical Tropical Gardens

Honolii Beach Park

Hilo Bay

Kaloko
Nat. Pk.

Puu
Waawaa

200

Wailuku River
State Park

Hualalai
8,271'

Hilo

Carlsmith
Beach Park

Kailua

Puu Huluhulu
Trail

Puu Oo
Horse Trail

11

Kona

Holualoa

Mauna Loa
Observatory

Moutnain
View

Lava Trees
State Park

Keahhou
Kuamoo Battlefield

11

130

Cook Monument

Captain Cook

Mauna Loa
13,679'

Makaala
Tree FernTrail

Kahaualea
Rain Forest

Pahoa

Puna

Kealakekua
Bay

Honaunau

Volcano

Kapoho
(Champagne)
Cove

Puuhonua O Honaunau
National Park

Hawaii
Volcanoes

Kilauea
Caldera

Chain of Craters

Kehena-Pohoiki
Scenic Coast

National
Park

Pu Loa
Petroglyphs

Ainipo
Trail

Milolii
Honomalino Beach

Kau Forest
Reserve

Wood
Valley

Pahala

Punaluu
(Black Sand)
Beach

Manuka
State Park

Naalehu

11

Ocean
View

N
W   E
S

South
Point

Byodo-In Temple, Oahu; Waipoo Falls, Kauai; Kehena Black Sand Beach, Puna, Big Island; Makaha beach boy, Oahu

Part Two

Da Plan!

Da Plan!

Puuhonua O Honaunau National Park, Big Island

WHIP OUT THE CREDIT CARD AND
MAKE YOUR VACATION HAPPEN

PART TWO

Of course the exact quote was "Da plane! Da plane!" uttered weekly on TV's Fantasy Island by the diminutive Tattoo (Herve Villechaize) to his boss, Mr. Roarke (Ricardo Montalban), as a new guests landed by seaplane at the mysterious island, where all manner of quirky, long-held dreams were fulfilled. The real-life location was Kaua'i's Allerton Garden, just one of the places your dreams can come true. And though a plane is part of your plan, first comes finding a place to stay. Then you need the plane ride, probably a rental car, and a packed suitcase.

LITTLE GRASS SHACK OR GRANITE COUNTERTOPS?
How to score the accommodations you want at the best price.

PACKAGE VACATIONS

One way of shortcutting the planning process is to book a package deal— room, plane, car. To find package deals, see the listings in the *Wiki-Wiki Phonebook*, page 141, talk to a travel agent, or review offerings in your Sunday newspaper's travel section or online. Some companies specialize in package vacations. Popular airlines, such as Hawaiian and United also offer vacation packages. Then there are the online brokers such as Orbitz, Travelocity, Priceline, Expedia, and Hotels.com. **Tips:** Even if choosing to buy a package, make sure to find out your specific resort and review it independently. Also get your flight itinerary to see if it calls for wasting hours making connections.

Quoted rates are normally "per person, based on double occupancy." Package accommodations usually feature mid- to higher-priced hotels at a resort strip. Booking a package deal doesn't mean you'll be herded around on a bus from a 30-foot pineapple statue to trinket shops at the mall. Once in Hawaii, you will be free to roam.

Package deals are there because brokers can get good rates booking planeloads of people at a time. You will almost always stay in a tourist zone and bookings are commonly for a week.

Money saver: After pricing a package vacation, get separate quotes for airline tickets and a car. Then add those figures and subtract from the package cost. Divide what remains by the number of nights included in your package: This figure is the rate you're paying per night, which you can try to beat when booking your own accommodations.

FINDING AND BOOKING YOUR OWN ACCOMMODATIONS

About seven million people visit the islands yearly, spread fairly evenly over the calendar, though summers and the Christmas holidays see an up tick. If you are looking for off-season rates and smaller crowds, try fall or spring, making sure to avoid Easter break, which also draws visitors—including local kids who are out of school and may have a notion of sharing a beach with you midweek, of all the nerve. **Money Saver:** Travel during non-peak seasons.

In a perfect world, you will find a place about three to six months before your trip. Both resort chains and owner-owned rentals want to get some of the calendar filled in and they will do so by offering better prices. As dates draw near, and occupancy rises, the law of supply and demand kicks in. Conversely, you impulsive types can find deals at the spur of the moment, when resorts must either rent the room or it goes vacant. **Money Saver:** Book three to six months in advance for better rates. Or try your luck if you're ready to leave tomorrow or the day after.

Price will be a consideration for most visitors. You can drop down thousands a night on bungalows at the Fairmont Orchid or ten bucks for

finding and booking your own accommodations, cont'd—

a beach camping permit. How important is your room? Do you want a place where you can wake up slowly and hang around? Or are you looking for a bed and shower to come back to after being out from dawn to dusk? **Money Saver:** If you plan active days away from your resort, then there's less sense in spending on the best accommodations.

You will generally get what you pay for when booking a room or cottage. By not eating out, paying pricey admissions to attractions, and by foregoing expensive tours, a couple can save $1,500 to $2,000 on a two-week vacation. That savings can then be applied to a higher-end rental. **Money Saver:** Save money on eating, attractions, and tours, and then splurge on your accommodations.

All accommodations charge a premium for oceanfront and ocean view. Many people want to admire the ocean from their rooms. But bear in mind that most of the time in your room will be spent sleeping. Garden views, as they are called, will be out of the salt spray and you will hear the ocean. Farther inland, you will get birdsong as a respite from the ocean's white noise. **Money Saver:** Non-oceanfront rooms are cheaper. You'll still hear the ocean with a garden view.

HUNT 'EM DOWN
After completing the armchair voyage in this book, you'll know which island you want to visit, for how long, and which locales are most appealing. Within that locale, further narrow the choice by deciding on a specific type of accommodation, i.e., resort, hotel, condominium, or cottage/home. Now it's time to start hunting.

1. Use the WikiWiki Phonebook, page 138, for specific accommodations in your chosen locale.

2. Call agents listed in the WikiWiki Phonebook and get them working for you.

3. Call friends you know who have been to Hawaii and get their opinions.

4. Get on the Internet. The great thing about the Internet, aside from being comprehensive and instantaneous, is photographs. Look both at what's shown and what's not shown. Some photos are framed to keep certain aspects out of the picture. Many listings include photos of places that are miles away from the accommodations. The text of the listing will also require interpretation. For instance, "cozy" may mean "tiny," "rustic" perhaps "dumpy," and the mentioning of "all new doormats," or "brand new towel racks," indicates a lack of anything better to say about the place.

An excellent website to find accommodations is VRBO—Vacation Rentals By Owner. Islands are organized by locale, with adjacent locales noted. Condominiums, guest rooms, cottages, and homes will be listed. You should compose an inquiry email, which you can copy and paste quickly into the VRBO listings that look good.

Keep a list and shotgun out many inquiries in a short time. Personalize your email to make yourself sound likeable and desirable, which of course you are. For instance, "we are returning to Hawaii for our tenth wedding anniversary," or "we're bringing grandpa back to the islands," or "it's been our lifelong dream to visit Hawaii." VRBO emails go to real people who want a good relationship with their prospective tenants.

You can also scare up tons of other Internet listings by searching for "Maui country cottage rentals," or "Big Island condominium vacations," or "vacation rental agents Hawaii." Go nuts. Sift through. You're only looking for one or two.

5. Local newspapers also have an online presence. In the classifieds you will find vacation rental listings.

6. Internet-based agencies like Hotels.com, Orbitz, Expedia, and Travelocity will have Hawaii listings. Beware of making a booking until you know, and can review, the exact lodging you want. Also note cancellation policies, which are normally stringent after you give them your credit card number. **Tip:** *You may be able to get a deal, especially if you are near your departure date.*

7. Visitors bureaus. Hawaii spends a fortune attracting visitors. Each island has a visitors bureau with an 800 number where you can obtain free information. You'll want to go online and further check these places, but it's a good place to start. You may even get personal recommendations from whomever answers the phone.

CHECK 'EM OUT

Narrow the results of your hunt down to a few possibilities. Now go back online to take a critical look at your selection. Search the Internet for the place names specifically and look for reviews and comments by previous guests. Some good sources online are Tripadvisor.com, E-pinions, About.com, hotels.com, and concierge.com.

THEN ASK THE RIGHT QUESTIONS

After the hunt and online background check, you will have narrowed the field to your personal darlings, which jive with your calendar, desires, and your wallet. At that point, it pays to contact the accommodations you've chosen and ask the right questions.

Beginning the questioning with emails works well, since you then have documentation of what has transpired. But before completing the transaction call to speak to someone on site. Many resorts are part of a chain, and you'll start out speaking to someone in Albuquerque. Get the local Hawaiian number. You'll make a personal connection (getting a name is good) and will be able to make your special requests. Talking on the phone is a sure way to find out if your resort has aloha. You'll be surprised, in most cases, how friendly people are in Hawaii and usually you'll have to slow down to talk to them. If the hotel seems curt or rushed or in any way gives you a bad vibe: forgeddaboutit. Find someplace that makes you feel welcome and good about going. **Tip:** Making a phone call is a way to read the 'aloha meter' of your accommodations.

The questions to ask will vary among visitors, depending on what's important. Here are some queries to consider:

1. Is the room quiet? Will I hear televisions, music, traffic, barking dogs? Is the room over the pool (which tends to be noisier)? In mountain zones on Kauai and Maui, roosters can be a bother. On the Big Island, you don't want to be around coqui frogs.

2. How recently was the room built/renovated?

3. Non-smoking? Are there mold or mildew smells? (This is the tropics; if you are pariculary bothered let them know and you usually will get an honest answer.)

4. What floor is the room on? (Top floor is generally more quiet. Disabled persons or families with small children may perfer ground floor.)

5. Does the room share walls with others rooms? (End units and units without common walls are more desirable.)

6. How large is the room or cottage? Bathtub, shower?

7. How close is the nearest neighbor/building? What is the view?

9. Do you have a … ? (Many places will list features, such as coffee maker, fridge, but make sure to check the specifics since they're not all the same.)

10. Do you have WiFi or Internet connections?

11. How close is the … beach, parking lot, whatever? (If you want to walk to the beach, is it through a shopping mall or across a garden to the sand?)

Tip: Once you arrive in Hawaii, you are not stuck in the room they put you in. Check the place out (realizing you are tired from the trip and might be picky) and if something isn't right, head back to the front desk. Hospitality people will try to make the dissatisfied (but polite) visitor happy.

HOW MUCH?

After securing your lodging, the time has come to pay for it. If you are booking into a large hotel or resort chain, you will first be quoted the "rack rate." Ask about promotional rates and special offers. Come right out and ask, "Is that the best you can do?" Smaller hotels may also have promotional rates. In addition, Hawaii has lower

finding and booking your own accommodations, cont'd—

rates for locals called the "Kama'aina" rate, which is about 20 percent off retail. If you have lived in Hawaii, you can ask for this rate. Hawaii residents can sometimes get a Kama'aina rate for visiting friends. If you are visiting Hawaii for anything that could be construed as a business purpose, you can also ask for a business traveler's discount. **Money Saver:** It never hurts to ask for a lower rate or special offering. Make sure all taxes are included in your nightly rate.

Money Saver: Before you sign on the dotted line, see if you can get them to hold the reservation for a few days. This minor delay will allow you some flexibility in booking your airline flight, where jogging a day or two can save money.

Money Saver: The longer you stay at one place, the cheaper your nightly rate will be. For instance, for a monthly booking, you can usually expect a 25-percent discount, or greater. This is particularly true for owner-rented properties.

Money Saver: Larger groups save money on accommodations. For instance, two couples can rent a two-bedroom house or condo for much less per person than one couple can rent a one-bedroom or smaller house.

THE MINI-ORDEAL OF TRANSPACIFIC FLIGHT

Most Hawaii flights include a stopover in Honolulu, a shuttle bus ride (the wikiwiki or "quick-quick") to the inter-island terminal, and then a brief flight to the outer islands. Flights to Honolulu from the West Coast take five-plus hours, not including check-in and X-ray at departure. Add in connecting flights in the U.S. and inter-island flights, and a 10- to 15-hour travel day is possible—if everything goes as planned.

Hawaiian, United, American, Alaska, Continental, and Delta are among the top mainland-to-Hawaii carriers. Hawaiian covers inter-island flights, and other airlines have partnership deals with them. New inter-island carriers come along occasionally, such as Go! Airlines, and offer cut-rate flights. Hawaiian commonly has the best on-time ratings, and will offer most flexibility for longer stays in the islands; they mainly fly to Honolulu and connect with inter-island flights. Their food and reservation services, however, have recently shown a decline in quality.

United and American offer outer-island-direct flights from the larger West Coast airports, which works well if you live near one of them.

Diamond Head and Waikiki, Oahu

Time saver: Take a good look at your itinerary and eliminate as many stopovers as possible. Some airlines have direct flights to outer islands from the mainland. By selecting carefully you can save eight or more hours of roundtrip travel time—almost one day of a two-week vacation.

Money Saver: Airline fares will vary greatly, depending on the day of your departure and the idiosyncratic pricing policies of the industry. You can save as much as 50 percent by picking the right day. Go online and noodle around a day or three on either side of your proposed departure. When you call the airline to get a quote, ask about promotional offers and also ask the booking agent to check on the days around your proposed departure date.

WHEELS
Most everyone traveling to Hawaii will want to rent a car. The exception might be Waikiki, where cars can be an outright inconvenience. Shuttles offer rides from the airport to Waikiki. A trolley services the Waikiki area, with connections to Honolulu, a few miles away. Shuttle buses and city buses will get you to Pearl Harbor, Polynesian Cultural Center, and Hanauma Bay for snorkeling. Beaches, shopping, and nightlife are within walking distance of Waikiki. Bicycles and motorbikes are available for rent. Still, if you want to see the rest of Oahu—and there's lots to see—a car will be needed. **Tip:** Check whether your hotel has free parking if staying in Waikiki.

Hawaii has more rental cars sprinkled into everyday traffic (about one in three or four) than any other state, and all major companies have a presence. Alamo frequently has the best deals and offers excellent service, but check around. The rental car decision is based mainly on lowest price. Give all the majors a call. Advertisements claim that lower prices are available online, but that's not always the case. You will want to go to the online stores to make sure—both the brokers, like Travelocity and Orbitz, and the websites of the car companies themselves. The good thing is that car rental companies will hold a reservation for free until the day of your arrival. **Tip:** Make sure your quote includes all additional charges and taxes, which are considerable.

Money Saver: Prices for rental cars fluctuate mysteriously. Call again before your vacation and you may well snag a better price. You can also often get a larger car, if you're interested, for little increase in price, since higher gas prices have lessened the demand for larger vehicles.

Money Saver: Look for specials in the travel section of Sunday newspapers, which will note a special code. Also, memberships, such as Costco and AAA, will earn a discount of five percent.

Rental car companies used to strong-arm customers at the counter into buying daily insurance, CDW, or collision damage waiver. The incentive was that if you hit a bug you would spend the rest of your days cooling your heels in a Hawaiian jail until you could pay cash for the car. Nowadays, they just make you check off boxes saying you decline. It's a good idea to bring a copy of your proof of insurance with you, though it is rarely needed. **Money Saver:** Check your insurance coverage before you leave or call your broker. If you have full coverage at home you will very likely have full coverage on your rental car and should not pay for additional coverage.

To four-wheel or not to four-wheel? With the exception of a red convertible, nothing says "tourist" like a red Jeep. You don't need a four-wheel drive on Oahu or Maui, though Maui has some roads where a very skinny car would be nice. Most of the dirt-road driving on Kaua'i can be done in a passenger vehicle, but a four-wheel drive is useful for forestlands below Waialeale, the spur Napali roads, and forest roads of Koke'e State Park. Adventuresome repeat visitors may want that traction in Kaua'i. On the Big Island, getting to the top of Mauna Kea requires four-wheel drive, as does driving down to Waipio Valley. But tours are available for both Mauna Kea and Waipio, where you can also walk in 20 minutes. A number of coastal roads and Mana Road around Mauna Kea on the Big Island require four-wheel drive. Though not necessary, the Big Island is most appropriate for four-wheel drive. Ironically, some major rental agencies rent Jeeps, etc., but then have restrictions that negate their practical use. Ask them. Or rent from Harpers, which specializes in SUVs and has few restrictions.

PACKLIST

Hawaii is hang loose. You will seldom if ever see a coat and tie, or gown with heels—except maybe in wedding parties. Record lows in Hawaii are mid-50s at sea level, and are normally in the 60s. Highs, winter and summer, will range from the higher 70s to mid-80s. In the morning, high elevations on the Big Island and Maui can be freezing, and Kaua'i's Waimea Canyon is often chilly in the morning.

SHOES

The essential footwear in Hawaii is none. Shoes are not worn in private homes.

Slippers (a.k.a flip-flops)
    Easy to buy here. Your driving-touring-all-around shoe Teva, Reef, Locals, Crocs, and other shoemakers make flip flops that have supportive, antibacterial footbeds, and a top strap that hugs the foot, thus taking some of the flip from the flop.
Airplane & dress-up shoe
    (athletic shoe, sandals, boat shoe)
Low-cut hiking shoes or cross-trainers
    Heavy hiking boots are too much, unless you're backpacking. Count on getting your trail shoes wet and muddy. These can double as your airplane shoe.
Surf shoe (bootie style, optional)
    Can be your beach-hiking choice. Good for reef walks and close-in swimming, especially on the Big Island, which has more rocky entries and tide pools. Also good for boulder hopping along Kaua'i's coast.

CLOTHING

Khaki pants plus aloha shirt or polo shirt
    (men, for plane and dress-up)
Dress or two piece: top + skirt or lightweight three-quarter or ankle-length pants
    (women, for plane and dress-up)
Cargo shorts (one or two pair, lightweight)
    Extra pockets provide quick reach for do-dads like lip balm and bug spray
Short sleeve tops (3 or 4, quick-dry synthetic)
    It takes forever for cotton to dry. For hiking, pick bright colors or white, which can be seen from a distance.

Long sleeve tops
    (two quick dry synthetic, or one synthetic and one light fleece)
    In early morning you'll want something more than a T-shirt
Gore-Tex shell or windbreaker
    You should plan for rain. A poncho is a low-cost way to beat the rain. On the high elevations of Big Island and Maui, and early morning at Koke'e State Park on Kauai, temps can be downright chilly and you'll want to layer all of the above.
Gore-Tex pants (optional)
    If you want to hike at higher elevations the pants add a degree of comfort and safety. The full suit also adds protection if you get caught out at night or in a down-pour.
Sun hat
    Either the full-blown wide-brim hat, or, to escape that fashion statement, wear a light weight billed hat and cover your face with plenty of sun block.
Fleece stocking cap and gloves (optional)
Sunglasses
Swimming suit
    Easy to buy in Hawaii. Men wear the longer board short; women's suits vary, but the boxy-bottom two-piece is popular.
Sarong to wrap around waist
    (women, optional beachwear)
Rash guard (optional, men and women)
    A synthetic Spandex, short sleeve stretch top worn while in the water for sun protection and warmth. Buy in Hawaii.

GEAR

Hiking pole *(retractable, optional)*
   Very useful on Hawaii's steep, slick trails, and for stream crossings and beating down spider webs. Also helpful to probe thick greenery for footing.

Snorkeling gear *(mask, snorkel, fins)*
   Gear can be purchased cheaply in Hawaii at Long's, Wal Mart, etc. (People who wear glasses can have prescription lenses attached inside, which of course you'll want to take care of at home.)
   Fins with heel straps that will accommodate your surf shoe are good for rocky entries and the snorkel-hikes to offshore islands. Rentals are also available and may be cheaper if you only snorkel a day or two. Also pick up some mask de-fogger, which comes in a little squeeze bottle and works better than spit.

Retractable umbrella *(for shade and rain, optional)*
   Easy to pack. Can be a smart choice on the right occasion.

Camera

Cell Phone
   Coverage is not available everywhere, but almost. A cell phone to call 911 in an emergency makes all the difference.

DAYPACK

Organize your daypack so that it can be used not only for hiking and beach use, but also as a "purse" that you can drag with you everywhere, thereby leaving your car free of valuables.

Antibiotic ointment
   Little cuts linger in the tropics.
Band Aids *(add gauze pads and athletic tape)*
Bandana
   For sun protection, towel, napkin.
Hydrogen peroxide in small squeeze bottle
   (optional, to wash cuts)
LED Flashlight or headlamp
   Plus extra batteries.
Food *(energy bar, jerky, snack mix)*
   In addition to packed lunch. Good for big and little emergencies.
Ibuprofen *(or other pain tablets and other medications you use)*
Mosquito repellant *(needed more in summer)*
Sunscreen/lip balm
Swiss Army knife
Towelettes *(pre-moistened, purse size)*
Water *(drink at least two liters per day)*
Water pump or water treatment tablets *(optional)*
   Do not drink stream water in Hawaii.

Maui Swap Meet

Maui conch blower, Sunset Beach lookout, Oahu; Monk seal, Kauai

PART THREE

*The Elements
of Island
Style*

On the Kalalau Trail, Kauai

WHAT TO DO AND NOT TO DO
WHEN YOU GET TO HAWAII

PART THREE

THE SEVEN STAGES OF ALOHA

A two- or three-week visit to Hawaii can be a life-changing experience, as well as a rocking good time.

People really do say "aloha" in everyday speech in Hawaii. Aloha means good-bye, hello, compassion, love—all of that. The word derives from the Hawaiian words "alo," meaning front or face, and "ha" meaning the essence or the breath of life. As in ancient times, some Hawaiians today will touch foreheads saying, "alo," and then breathe out saying "ha," thus exchanging life's breath. Don't worry, this isn't something expected of you at the car rental counter. But you may well feel the aloha by the end of your stay in Hawaii, so don't be afraid to say it. Aloha is Hawaii's gift to the world, not a souvenir you need to buy; it will seek you if you are interested.

STAGE ONE: **BEFUDDLEMENT**

Months and perhaps years of expectation have just endured the daylong whirlwind-and-doldrums of airports, baggage claims, and lines. Your underwear is ill-fitting and you are dehydrated. You have arrived. Small quirks in your room's appointments loom as major setbacks. Have a cocktail immediately and put your bare feet in the warm Pacific.

STAGE TWO: **INACTMENT**

The day rises and you're in Hawaii. Equip your day pack and get the car organized. Next come trips to the stores to stock up on all the stuff and beach gear. This is a preparation day, as your mind catches up to your body. Find a quiet place for afternoon and sunset. Repeat the end of Stage One.

STAGE THREE: **EXPERIENCE**

Now come the Oh Wows. A half-day on the trail or sightseeing, and a half-day at the beach. Your head fills with new images of the islands. You're looking forward now, and see no end. Stages One and Two are jettisoned.

STAGE FOUR: **IMMERSION**

Repeat Stage Three. Different sides of the island, the gardens, waterfalls, reefs and beaches, the museums, restaurants, and historical sites. You keep taking them in. It's a bit overwhelming. Was that just yesterday?

STAGE FIVE: **REACTION**

After days of immersion, you begin to shed your skin. Your body has cycled through, literally taking in the molecules of Hawaii with each breath and swallow and footstep. You have nicks, bites, and sunburn. This bodily reaction naturally follows immersion.

STAGE SIX: **CONNECTION**

Somewhere, it happens. You're not thinking about it. At this moment you feel all the forces of nature working dynamically, harmoniously, infinitely. It's always this way, but you have just noticed. You hear the rustle above and look up to see light on the banana leaves. You always knew it would be like this, but you could not have anticipated the feeling. Stage Six, in some cases, will be accompanied by Going Native, i.e., tying a sarong around your head and having a gin fizz with breakfast because why not? Or taking a dip in the moonlight for the same reason.

STAGE SEVEN: **ALOOOOOOOOOOOO-HA!**

You get it. You have come to know these remarkable people, the Hawaiians, and how they lived for centuries with respect for the aina, the land, and with a sense of sharing for all eternity. You know this is a Pollyannaish historical view, but it seems now like a beacon for the future, for your future. This realization of aloha, in some cases, will be followed by the corollary, Let's Buy Real Estate.

THE EIGHTH STAGE...

As any Hollywood screenwriter will tell you, the trick to creating high drama is to build a "ticking clock" into the plot. In many cases this is a literal clock, a time bomb, but more often it's the upcoming date of the big game, the waning days before the disease is fatal, the deadline set by a mobster, the day that the parents get home, and so on. On the movie of your vacation, the ticking clock that creates high drama is the hour of your departure. The feeling of aloha—let's get away and live here forever, what's life for anyway? —is heightened by the fact that you have to leave.

Before you sell the ranch and move, consider renting for a while. The eighth stage of aloha, with no time limit to create dramatic tension, is wide-ranging and can include island fever, personal fulfillment, dread of mosquitoes, mildew and termites, and longing for the mainland. Hawaii has seen 'em all.

Poipu Beach, Kauai

MAKING A GOTTA-DO-IT LIST

Who wants to goose-step to a schedule during a vacation? It is a vacation, after all. On the other hand, you do want to have a grab bag full of activities in mind, and some idea of when is the best time to do them.

One way to get minimally organized is to draw up a calendar (or use a daytimer) to keep track of date-specific activities. Also, make up a Gotta-Do-It list of what you want do before you leave, for which dates are flexible but weather is a prime consideration. For example, heading to the highest peaks can mean heading into a storm, so it's best to go on a blue-sky day; similarly, visit the windward (rainy) sides of the island when it's sunny, and use visits to the leeward shore as a fall-back when it is raining.

Tips for making the Gotta-Do-It list

— Pick out the most enticing entries from the Best Of categories. These are the things that attracted you in the first place, your Gotta-Have-Its.

— Read the local newspapers and tourist publications, and listen to local radio, to find what events are going on during your stay. Add these to your calendar.

— Look at TOUR$ OR INDEPENDENT TRAVEL in this section, and decide which, if any, of the tours seem right for you and your travel mates. Add these to your Gotta-Do-It list, and to the calendar once you've made reservations.

As your vacation progresses, check stuff off the list, and add other items. Stay flexible.

PICKING AN ISLAND STYLE

You and your travel mates are free to do what you want. And the other 50,000 people visiting the island can do what suits them, too. Some of them may end up wanting to do the same thing you are, and at the same time, since tourists wake up with a job to do—to have fun in a large-but-limited space. You may wind up spending unplanned time in traffic jams and crowds and, therefore, may not wind up doing exactly what you want—unless you anticipate.

Each island has its predicable flow. On Maui, the cars stream up Haleakala and onto the Hana Highway in the early to mid-morning, and then line up to get back to Ka'anapali or Kihei in the late afternoon. On Oahu, where tourism is less evident, since 1.2 million locals are also scurrying about, you will nonetheless see tourist pileups at Pearl Harbor and Hanauma Bay during the morning. On Kaua'i, Ke'e Beach on the Napali Coast can be clogged at 10 a.m. and the Waimea Canyon turnouts receive the conga line of rental cars about the same time. On the Big Island, Kona gets heavily bogged with beachgoers on the sundown rebound from South Kohala beaches.

Putt-putting along in a line of traffic in a rental car is not a bad thing in Hawaii, watching the sun go down on the Pacific, and so on. Over a two-week vacation, however, spending an extra hour or two each day putt-putting along translates to nearly two days' worth of your waking hours that you could spend doing something else. Some days you will avoid this issue by walking from your bed to the nearest beach or pool and staying put. On other days, when you want to get out and about, you may want to be aware of what kind of "bird" you are.

THE THREE SPECIES OF HAWAIIAN TOURIST BIRDS:

EARLY BIRD
We're not talking worms. Instead you are out early, coffee and breakfast in hand, and lunch in a bag. How early? Well, before eight if you're on the Big Island and headed to the other side, but a little before eight on the other islands—late enough not to be in the school-commute traffic. (The Early Bird Extremis will get out before the workers.) For many visitors, the thought of not sleeping in on vacation will be ... not a vacation. Others will want to grasp the opportunity. Bear in mind that Hawaii is two or three (during daylight savings) hours behind Pacific time, that is, 7 a.m. in San Francisco is 5 a.m. in Honolulu, or 4 a.m. during daylight savings. So, your body will be waking up earlier anyway.

Early Birds will be ahead of the curve all day long. You will see the island in beautiful morning light—a big plus—and come upon beaches, trails, and scenic overlooks in virtual solitude, absorbing the sights and sounds of nature. In a few hours the same spots will be receiving the bulge of tourists and tour busses. Some of these places will be hardly recognizable as you pass them again on the return leg of your day. You are back earlier, doing the end-of-day, pre-dinner routine at your leisure.

THE B-a-L-D EAGLE
The Bald Eagle, aside from being patriotic, builds the day around breakfast, lunch, and dinner (B, L, D). Slow mornings blend into breakfast. Morning activities precede lunch. In the afternoon, activities take place until it's time to get back, take a shower, and head out to dinner. Beaches, trails, and the parking lots of attractions start to fill up at mid-morning (based on the majority of

people getting going between 9 and 10 in the morning) and start to empty out between 3:30 and 5 in the afternoon.

Bald Eagles are normal, statistically speaking. Most of us are Bald Eagles. We spend more time looking for parking spaces and waiting in lines.

THE NIGHT OWL
The Night Owl is the flip side of the Early Bird. The Night Owl lingers in the morning, does something locally, and takes off at the lunch lull, behind the Bald Eagles who are well on their way. True, the Night Owl gets places behind the curve, into the thick of things on occasion. But the owls roost in late afternoon, staying put while the crowds start to head home. The Night Owls rule sunset. Some great snorkeling and hiking can be done during these later hours. Having dinner on the beach—from a local takeout or as a picnic—is a reserved seat in the most beautiful restaurant in the world.

The Night Owls will be driving home in the dark or dusk, missing out on scenery, but they will be doing so when locals and vacation commuters alike have already made the trip and are settling into their homes and restaurants for the evening. The Night Owl may finish the day doing the type of carousing we expect of this species, or with a quieter moonlight stroll, before going to sleep in anticipation of getting up late and doing it again.

ON WEEKENDS and holidays, you may want to chicken out and be an ostrich (enough bird-brained metaphors!). Hawaiians love their beach parks and their forest reserves, so the throngs basically double up. Pick activities close to your accommodation. Or, pick a less popular destination and be early, since working people here will sleep in on the weekend just like on the Mainland.

TOUR$ OR INDEPENDENT TRAVEL

While it is true that the best things in tropical life are free, it is also true that in Hawaii a large industry is built around enhancing your vacation for a price. What are the tour choices, how much do they cost, and are they worth it?

Once you step off the plane, and later as you walk through shopping centers and hotel lobbies, you will see racks brimming with promotional cards and free tourist publications. Acquire a stack for perusal at your leisure. In the free publications you will see ads for many of the tour companies, often with special offers. Also, at shopping centers you will see kiosks manned by an activities broker, who can make bookings (and invite you to a timeshare sales pitch). **Money Saver:** Tour companies are competitive. Do not pay full retail for a tour. Activities brokers offer discounts, hotels concierges offer deals, and coupons are printed in the tourist publications.

The Internet will also be very helpful in researching tours. You will find websites ranging from hokey one-pagers of sole proprietors to many-leveled, flashy jobs offering multiple tours on multiple islands. For getting information, you're better off going to the website of the actual company, rather than a site brokering many different companies. A quick search online ("Maui snorkel tour," "Mauna kea tour," or whatever) will quickly make finite what seems to be an overwhelming variety of options. **Money Saver:** After you've located your tour, you will be able to book online for a 10- to 20-percent discount.

General Tips for all tours: Ask about cancellation policies to make sure you won't be on the hook in bad weather. Some adventure tours exclude children, or have height and weight limitations, but most welcome children, at prices discounted about 20 percent. Many tours, particularly on Oahu, offer hotel pickup, but most will require driving to a set point. Find out how much drive time from the pick-up point is included in your tour. Also ask about reservation requirements: Often you'll be better off waiting for the ideal weather (sea, wind, rain) and booking that day or the day before. On most tours, a gratuity for the guide is expected. See Wiki-Wiki Phonebook, page 137, for tour operators.

Kalihiwai Bay, Kauai

SURFING LESSONS

In Hawaii, surfing is the sport of kings, with a centuries-old tradition. No experience is necessary, since almost everyone who takes lessons is a novice. The best deal is a group lesson, usually for three to six people. Two hours (as long as you'll probably have enough energy) costs between $50 and $75. For private lessons, figure about $100 to $150. You can also find multi-day lessons for several hundred dollars and full-fledged surf camps and schools for a couple thousand. Larger outfitters that employ a team of instructors give most surfing lessons. But don't be hesitant to retain a sole-proprietor operating out of the back of his truck. Oahu has the most surf lessons (Waikiki and the North Shore), but Maui (Lahaina, Kihei), and Kauaʻi (Hanalei Bay, Poipu Beach) also offer excellent opportunities. **Tips:** Make sure your instructor is state-licensed and lifeguard-trained. Many lessons guarantee that they'll get you standing or the lesson is free, so ask. Also make sure a rash guard (protective shirt) comes with the lesson.

Is it worth it? For sure, dude. Even if you have experience, local guys will supply a board and a place to ride waves where tourists are welcomed. Prices are right and it's a bona fide Hawaiian experience and a thrill.

SAILING AND CRUISES

The Hawaii of antiquity was founded upon the journeys of outrigger sailing canoes. Today you will find a smorgasbord of opportunities to discover the offshore waters. Cruises offer whale watching, sightseeing, sunset viewing, and snorkeling (covered below). Dinner cruises are available, but think twice, since eating and ocean swells can combine to make seasickness. Boats range from large, single-hulled cruisers with a 100 or more passengers, to 60-foot catamaran sailboats with a few dozen passengers, to hard-bottom rubber rafts skimming through the waves with a half-dozen passengers. If you really want to sail—as in wind for fuel—be sure to get that straight, since most sailboats motor.

Tips: In general, the larger the boat, the less apt you will be to get seasick. Envision what size of craft seems right, and then check out a photo online or go look in person.

On the Big Island, most of the action is out of Kona, on large boats for sunset cocktail cruises and excursions. On Oahu, vessels depart mainly from Ala Wai Harbor near Waikiki; some depart from Waianae on the rough-and-tumble West Side of the island, about an hour's drive away. The romantic seaport of Lahaina on Maui offers scads of cruising opportunities, along with the ferries to outer islands of Molokai and Lanai. Kihei also has a harbor. On Kaua'i, drab Port Allen is the take off for almost all cruises, including all those to the Napali Coast. Although craft options are many, prices are fairly consistent. For longer tours, about 4 hours, expect to pay $85 to $110. Two-hour cruises run from $60 to $80, on average. Less expensive (under $50) are also available for quickie offshore soirees: Several depart Waikiki on Oahu. (A moonlight-night cruise off Waikiki is quite a sight.) At Lahaina on Maui, you can take a shorter trip out for $25 to $45; on Kaua'i, check out Waimea for a short whale-watching excursion, for about $40. Sometimes shorter is better.

Tips: Check reservation policies. You can often book a cruise at short notice, on a day with optimum wave and weather conditions. Weather may mean the difference between being on a dream cruise or a puke boat.

Is it worth it? Aye matey, but this is a personal choice, worth it for those who know they enjoy the open seas. Other visitors can equivocate: You can see sunsets, whales, waves, and other islands from dry land. The value is there, since you ride an expensive craft with trained crew. You get a shared experience with fellow passengers. The weather will be a big factor in the experience.

SNORKELING

Another Hawaii is under the ocean's surface, in the sparkling blue-gold world of fish and coral reefs. As is the case with other cruises, the size of craft and number or passengers varies greatly among tours, and you'll want to hone in on one

that seems right. And, check the weather forecast or wait to make a reservation until a calm day. Some snorkel tours never hit the seas, but rather transport you in a van and then shore-dive at the locale. Prices range from about $60 to $75 for close-to-shore adventures of two or three hours, to $120 to $175 for longer runs to outer reefs, islands, and remote coastlines. **Tip:** The exact destination of your snorkeling site is also good to know. Many snorkeling tours go to places that intermediate-level snorkelers can reach from shore.

On Kaua'i, the best tours head for the Napali coast, particularly in summer, or 20 miles offshore to Lehua Island (next to Ni'ihau, the Forbidden Island). Maui's premier destination is tiny Molokini Island, a little crescent-shaped marine preserve a few miles offshore of Kihei; dozens of vessels and hundreds of snorkelers moor in the small bay. Other Maui destinations are Turtle Town, Oneuli (Black Sand) Beach, Olowalu, and Coral Gardens, all of which are reachable from shore. On the Big Island, a fleet of boats carrying hundreds of swimmers heads to the Captain Cook Monument at Kealakekua Bay; this spot is reachable on foot, via a semi-hard trail that drops down from near the highway. You can also rent kayaks and paddle a few miles to the monument. On Oahu, several tour companies depart Ala Wai Harbor or the piers at Aloha Tower, both fairly close to Waikiki. Other operators shuttle you from Waikiki to Waianae Harbor to visit West Side reefs, an adventure that will take about 3 hours, with only about 40 minutes in the water.

Is it worth it? Possibly, but the mask is foggy. Beginning snorkelers can find easy spots on shore to learn on all the islands. Snorkelers with experience can reach from the shore many locales tour companies use. So, unless you really want a sightseeing boat ride, snorkeling is something you can do on your own. Exceptions are reefs and islands farther offshore the main island. Visitors who want to try snuba or scuba diving will also want a guide. (Snuba, a cross between snorkel and scuba, is when divers hover below the surface in the fishiest of waters, breathing via a tube leading down from the surface vessel.)

Haleakala Crater (valley), Maui

SIGHTSEEING

Sightseeing bus rides are the most common, cheapest, and least "necessary" tours taken in Hawaii. Most visitors are transported by shuttle bus or full-sized bus by two major companies—Polynesian Adventure Tours and Roberts Hawaii. Many other smaller companies offer tours, including a host of have-van-will-guide sole proprietors. For the bigger buses and large companies, you can buy a tour for between $35 and $75. Small-time operators will cost more, around $75 to $100, and offer a more-personalized and colorful experience in exchange. Of course, bigger buses stick to a route and schedule, and make stops at establishments that have worked out a deal with the tour companies. In general, tour bus drivers are a friendly and well-informed lot.

Is it worth it? Not really, but it will be for some. Two people with a car ($25 to $35 a day) can grab a fistful of free tourist publications and create their own tour, hitting all the highlights. (Big Island's Mauna Kea is an exception; four-wheel drive required.) Dig a little deeper with a good guidebook and your own observations, and your day tour becomes an adventure. Sightseeing tours make the most sense for visitors who don't have a car, don't want to drive, and want to zone out listening to a narrative and have a shared experience with fellow travelers. Tours are also a way for a member of your party to go solo for the day.

HIKING

Each island has one or two premier hike-tour companies, often combining hikes with swims, snorkels, or zip-line adventures. Distances start at a couple miles or fewer ("hike-sees"). Full-day hikes are often only about six or seven miles. Cost, including van ride and lunch, isn't exactly cheap, ranging from about $75 to $150. Excursions hover in the magic $80 to $100 range. On Oahu you can get a cheapie hike for $20 or $30 to a close-in, heavily used trail, such as Manoa Falls, or downtown quickies out of Nu'uanu Valley to Kapena Falls and the Tantalus Trails.

Quite a few hiking tours use public trails (Haleakala National Park on Maui; Hawaii Volcanoes National Park and Waipio Valley on the Big Island; the above-mentioned trails and Diamond Head State Monument on Oahu; and Sleeping Giant, Waialeale "Blue Hole," and Waimea Canyon-Napali Trails on Kaua'i). But several hiking outfitters on all the islands go onto large private parcels, with special arrangements with the owners. (Princeville Ranch and Robinson land on Kaua'i; Ka'aawa Valley on Oahu; Kohala Ditch property on the Big Island; and mountain forests above Lahaina on Maui).

Tip: Find out your specific hike destination and distance. You may feel gypped to see other hikers doing the same thing for free. Private land hike tours will get you someplace you cannot otherwise go.

By special arrangement with smaller companies, you can take hikes where you really are better off with a guide. Examples are Oahu's highest peak, Mt. Ka'ala; high-altitude Mauna Loa and remote trails of southern Kona on the Big Island; the high elevations of Mt. Waialeale and Mt. Kawaikini on Kauai; and the Eke Trail and perhaps Kaupo Trail on Maui. These are tougher hikes with remote trailheads.

Is it worth it? Maybe, but the trail is sketchy. Many advertised hikes are easily achieved by hikers with average skill levels. You don't need special equipment. Other hikes are actually sightseeing tours with strolls built in here and there. The best values are private-property hiking tours or retaining a guide to take you someplace that is a real trek. One major upside to all hiking tours is the benefit of the guide's knowledge; even seasoned Hawaii hikers will pick up new tidbits about the flora, fauna, and history.

HELICOPTERS
To get up in the air for 45 to 90 minutes, you'll spend from $140 to $270, which seems like a lot. But considering it costs that much to talk to a lawyer or a shrink, and that you can't fly on your own, helicopter rides may be the best bang for your tour buck. (On Oahu you can get a quickie up and down for under $100.) Carriers are competitive, so prices are very similar. Still, shop the price, check out the number of years of operation, safety record, and years of experience of pilots. (In the 13 years from 1994 to early 2007, there were 11 crashes in all of Hawaii, involving 40 fatalities; hundreds of thousands of passengers have been flown.)

Also get them to tell you the specific flight plan and time in the air. You run through a safety check, a la commercial airlines, and then climb aboard and don a headset that carries peaceful music and the dulcet voice of the pilot.

Tips: If anyone is prone to airsickness, let the pilot know beforehand; if your group is up for more of a thrill ride, let them know that as well. *Note:* Most companies have an individual weight limitation of 250 pounds.

As is the case with boat cruises, you want to go up on a good day. Check out the reservation and cancellation policy of your operator. Check local weather forecasts and pick your day, or wait until

a clear day and make a last-minute booking. **Tip:** Taking a ride early in your vacation is a good way to scope out where you want to go.

Is it worth it? Roger that. You get a god's-eye overview of beautiful topography and seascapes. (Most rides on the Big Island only do a portion, normally Hawaii Volcanoes National Park; all-island tours will be around $400.) The experience is serene and it will give you a vacation within a vacation. Most people aren't ready to come down after a chopper ride. Then again, some visitors will balk at the expense and the thought of risking their necks in a whirlybird when they don't have to.

HORSEBACK RIDING
Aloha, pardner. Hawaiian cowboys—paniolos—were roping doggies decades before their American counterparts. The biggest private ranch in the U.S. is on the Big Island, and the first American rodeo champion was a Hawaiian. Horseback riding is not a gimmick here. Most trail rides are on big family ranches and led by people who know their horses. Other outfitters have leases to enter state forest reserves and parks, such as Haleakala on Maui. Though the outer islands will offer the most choices and variety, even Oahu has good riding, above North Shore and on the north Windward Coast. You can get in the saddle for 60 to 90 minutes for $60 to $80; for two hours to a half-day, expect to pay from $100 to $150. Trail rides are a good pick for the family, and children are cheaper, but height and age limitations will apply. See *Best Of* categories, page 132, for specifics on each island.

Tips: Get a good handle on the terrain you will cover and the length of the ride. You can choose from arid mountains, verdant pastures, forests reserves, and coastal bluffs. Ask the outfitter, or go online. Also find out (if you care) if you're on public land where you'll see hikers, or will be roaming a private ranch. Make sure you'll be covering enough distance to make it a real ride.

Is it worth it? Yup. Provided your rear-end and the horse's are compatible, horseback riding delivers the goods. You get an inside look at a real Hawaiian tradition.

KAYAKING

Kaua'i has Hawaii's only navigable waterways, some 10 rivers and streams, that usually (absent rain conditions) are lagoonlike for a half-mile to several miles inland. All these waterways are easy for beginners, though tours are licensed for only three rivers. The rest of the paddling in Hawaii is to small, nearby islands, inside protected reefs and bays, or along remote coasts, when the seas permit. If you're into kayaking, the choice really is whether to go on a guided tour or to rent a boat and rack and go it alone. Daily rentals for a single kayak range from $28 to $60, and doubles run about $45 to $80. Weekly rates are lower.

Tips: Find out if your "daily" rental is 8 hours or 24 hours. Make sure your quoted price includes all the "extras," like paddles, dry bags, car rack (if you don't rent at put in), and life vests. Note: A lot of people rent kayaks for non-guided paddles to Cook Monument across Kealakekua Bay; know that sea swell at Napo'opo'o Wharf often makes the put-in difficult. Local guys sometimes help out for tips, but ask your rental company about help at the put-in.

Many tours aren't all that much of a bump up from rental prices, with costs of $75 to $100 for the popular runs up Kauai's Wailua and Hanalei rivers; offshore Kailua on Windward Oahu and Waikiki; and out of Makena Landing on Maui. Prices jump to $125 to $200 or more for the long run to Kealakekua Bay on the Big Island; Napali Coast and the extended Poipu coast to Kipu Kai on Kaua'i; and the offshore waters from Keanae to Hana on Maui. **Tip:** When heading into open water, outside of bays and reefs, go with a guide. Some of the excursions—Napali comes to mind—can be true adventure-sport challenges. (See page 93 for more on kayaking.)

Is it worth it? Aye aye, with considerations. The value is there, in possessing an expensive kayak plus gear for a day. The experience is bona fide, leaving the land for a river lagoon, tiny island, or open coastline. You can pick your day, without a lot of planning. Tours are worth the extra if you're taking a real adventure. For safer waters and popular spots, many visitors will want to save money and have more fun by going it alone.

BICYCLING

The most popular bike tour in Hawaii is the ride down the 10,000-foot Haleakala Volcano on Maui. For between $60 and $130 (depending on the company and whether you start at the top or not) you can become one with a bicycle seat for up to 38 miles, often wearing a plastic suit and helmet while descending the paved road in traffic through fog, rain, and wind (yes, that's sarcasm). Many people enjoy this experience, the world's longest downhill glide. On Kaua'i you can find a similar experience, dropping down 4,000 feet and 12 miles from the rim of Waimea Canyon to Kekaha, with blue-water view of Ni'ihau most of the way.

Road cyclists can choose a whole different experience on the Big Island, where two or three companies offer week-long package tours with full support and accommodations included, from $2,500 to $3,000. You will find little between the two extremes—the thrill ride and the odyssey—although on Oahu John Alford's company offers tours in the Tantalus region above Waikiki. Biking doesn't lend itself to guided tours, since it's hard to narrate and keep the group together. But, there is some great cycling to be had in Hawaii (see Best Of, page 130). You can rent a bike for a day for between 10 and 30 bucks, even cheaper by the week.

Is it worth it? The best bet is to rent a bike—one of the best deals in the tour business. It's a great way to get around your resort area. Oahu's North Shore and Waikiki are fun on a bike, as are Hanalei, Kapa'a, and Poipu on Kaua'i. Both Kaua'i and the Big Island have many excellent trail and dirt track rides.

ATV TOURS

Now that the sugar cane industry has taken a dive (only two mills operate statewide), owners of large agricultural lands offer guided ATV rides as a way of augmenting income. Large ranches also shuffle in ATV adventures between horseback tours. Terrain varies among coastal bluffs, valley waterfalls, and high pastoral slopes. Most of the action on Kaua'i is around Koloa, where you ride through a long tunnel, and Kipu Ranch.

On Maui, rides take place mainly on the lower slopes of Haleakala (at 3,000 to 4,000 feet), and the Big Island's tours take place at Parker Ranch and the Kohala Mountains in the north. On Oahu, check out Kualoa Ranch on the northern Windward Coast. Plan on spending about $100 for a two-hour ride and $110 to $150 for rides of three or four hours. Some companies offer vehicles that will accommodate passengers, who pay $20 to $30 less than the driver.

Tips: Find out the distance of your tour so you don't spend excessive time listening to narratives as everyone parks with engines idling. Many tours offer lunch and clothing, since rides are often wet and muddy.

Is it worth it? For some people. You will get to see parts of the island not otherwise available, and you are supporting tourism that keeps these lands undeveloped. It's a tad pricey, compared to other tours, but if you're into ATVs, the value is there. Unlike other Hawaiian tours—sailing, surfing, kayaking—ATV riding is something that can be accomplished in the wide-open spaces of other Western States. And, with your trusty rental car you can drive to many mountainous and coastal scenic spots on Hawaii.

Princeville Ranch zipline, Crusing Napali coast, Kauai

LIVIN' LARGE FOR LESS

Beyond lodging and travel costs, the money spent on your vacation is largely discretionary. Couple-A can easily get rid of $2,000 to $3,500 over a two-week vacation on meals, admissions, incidentals, and tours. Couple-B can easily get by for under $500. Who gets the most enjoyment? Of course, all this comes down to personal preference and budget. Below are some ways to save.

A contrarian word: Spending is not a bad thing. Tourist dollars directed toward museum admissions, Hawaiian artwork, and eco-friendly businesses help support the economy built around preserving Hawaii's natural and cultural resources.

THE BEST IN HAWAIIAN LIFE IS FREE—Act like a local and head for beaches, beach parks, forest reserves, and scenic drives, which are Hawaii's priceless offering. Nature's gifts are the number-one reason people visit the state.

LIVING THE LUXURY—Destination resorts aren't just for well-heeled guests and conventioneers. Visitors are welcomed to peruse shops and restaurants. The best resorts are botanical gardens, museums, and architectural wonders all rolled into one (see *Best Of*, page 108). Public beach access facilities at resorts usually are better than at government-run beach parks. In the evenings, and also during the day, you may enjoy cultural events and entertainment.

HULA SHOWS—Resorts aren't the only place offering free entertainment. Shopping centers also schedule free shows. On Kaua'i, try Poipu Shopping Center, Kukui Grove in Lihue, and Coconut Marketplace in Wailua; on Maui, go to the Cannery Mall in Lahaina, Whaler's Village in Ka'anapali, or Queen Ka'ahumanu Center in Kahului; on the Big Island, check out the show at the Keahou Shopping Center, the ceremony preceding the luau at the Kona Pier, or shows at Hulihe'e Palace; on Oahu, pick from a number of Waikiki Resorts, and the Dole Shopping Center.

KLIP DA' KUPONS—Those free publications are full of special offers and two-fers on restaurant meals, admissions, and store purchases. Yes, they are a come-on, but stick to what's offered and you'll save.

BEACH CLUB PITCHES—If you're willing to kill ninety minutes listening to a timeshare presentation, you can get 100 bucks cash or coupons for free meals at good restaurants. (Or maybe you really are considering buying a timeshare.) Inquire at the resorts or at the booths of activities brokers.)

GARDENS AND ARBORETUMS—Many botanical gardens offer free admission. See *Best Of*, page 103.

WATCH SURFERS—Some of the best in the world ply their trade and spectators pay no admission. For the best places to watch surfers, see *Best Of*, page 91.

DINE ALA FRESCO—Skip the restaurants and buy food at local fruit and veggie stands. Local supermarkets, such as Big Save, Foodland, and Star, have take-out goodies and plate lunch specials. Pick a nice beach park for lunch or dinner and you will save a bundle, eat well, and have a table with a view.

CHURCHES—In Hawaii are a wealth of churches of many denominations and styles, and in magnificent settings. See *Best Of*, page 110.

GALLERIES, BOOKSTORES, VINTAGE AND HAWAIIANA SHOPS—Many shops are as good as museums. See *Walk-Around Tourist Towns* on page 105.

EVENTS AND CELEBRATIONS—Check with the Hawaii Visitors Bureau, the radio, and with local newspapers and publications for events. Art shows, canoe races, cultural gatherings, performances, and town celebrations are a good way to have free fun, local style. You'll find a lot going on at beach parks on the weekends.

NOTABLE FREEBIES—Not all museums, visitors centers, and attractions come with a price tag—though donations are appreciated. Here are some with no admission charge. Please see *WikiWiki Phonebook, page 137,* for phone numbers.

KAUAI
Fort Elizabeth State Park, Waimea
Guava Kai Plantation, Kilauea
Kaua'i Coffee Company Visitors Center, Port Allen
Kaua'i Hindu Monastery, Kapa'a
Kilohana Plantation, Lihue
Koke'e Natural History Museum
Sunshine Markets—Hanalei, Kilauea, Kapa'a, Koloa, Kekaha
Waioli Mission, Hanalei (walk the grounds)

OAHU
Ali'iolani Hale-Kawaiahao Church, Honolulu
Aloha Stadium Swap Meet, Honolulu
Aloha Tower, Chinatown, Honolulu
Army Museum, Waikiki
Duke's Canoe Club, Waikiki
Hawaii State Art Museum, Honolulu
Iolani Palace, Honolulu (walk the grounds)
Kahala Mandarin Dolphins
Kaneaki Heiau, Makaha
Mormon Temple, Laie
North Shore Surf & Cultural Museum, Haleiwa
Pacific Sky Diving Center, Mokuleia
Pu'u O Mahuka Heiau, Waimea
Punchbowl-National Memorial Cemetery of the Pacific
Royal Mausoleum, Honolulu
Top of Waikiki, Oceanarium, The Tube, Waikiki
Tropic Lightning Museum, Schofield Barracks
USS Arizona Memorial at Pearl Harbor

MAUI
Baldwin and Wing Ho museums, Lahaina
Hana Cultural Center
Humpback Whale National Marine Sanctuary, North Kihei
Lahaina Prison (Hale Pa'ahao)
Maui Nui Botanical Garden, Kahului
Maui Swap Meet, Kahului
Old County Building and Courthouse, Wailuku
Tedeschi Winery, Kula

BIG ISLAND
Amy Greenwell Ethnobotanical Gardens, Captain Cook
Danny Akaka's Talk Story, Mauna Lani Resort
Dolphin Quest, Hilton, Waikaloa
Hulihe'e Palace (walk the grounds)
Isaac Art Center, Waimea
Kaupulehu Cultural Center, Four Seasons
Kona coffee tasting: Royal Kona, Bayview, UCC Pacific Co-op
Kona Historical Society, Captain Cook
Lapakahi State Historical Park, Kawaihae
Mo'okini Heiau, Hawi
Mokupapapa Center for Hawaiian Reefs, Hilo
Onizuka Center for International Astronomy, Mauna Kea
Pu'ukohola Heiau Visitors Center, Kawaihae
Volcano Art Center, Jaggar Museum, Volcano House, Hawaii Volcanoes Visitors Center (park admission required)

HOW NOT TO HAVE A KILLER VACATION

Hawaii hosts nature's most violent events: hurricanes, volcanoes, tsunamis, and earthquakes. Yet today, thanks to enhanced forecasting and early-warning systems, few people are harmed.

When mother nature punches the ticket in Hawaii, she often does so on the nicest of days, in the prettiest of places, and when victims are least expecting. No one wants to think morbidly on their Hawaiian vacation, yet several tourists die monthly somewhere in the islands. Hawaiians feel genuinely bad about tragic accidents (which also happen to locals) and heroic efforts take place routinely to save people. Still, everyday a new batch of visitors gets off the jet, visions of travel-magazine paradise fresh in their minds, and clueless as to everyday dangers.

The goods news is that virtually all recreational-related fatalities are avoidable. Especially yours. Here are the five primary dangers and how to avoid them:

1. DROWNING

Among the ways to die while having fun in Hawaii, drowning is the most popular. Most frequently, drowning results from swimmers getting caught in, and then fatigued by, near-shore currents, a.k.a., riptides or rip current. Water coming ashore as waves must also recede, and it does so in many patterns, depending on the nuances of the shoreline. Every beach can be both perfectly safe and lethally dangerous, depending on the wave conditions of the day. The cardinal rule is that bigger waves mean stronger currents will be forming.

How not to drown: Pick a beach with a waterman (lifeguard)—many county beach parks have them—and don't be shy about asking advice. On all the islands you'll find swimming places where safety virtually is assured. But most adventurers will want to explore wild beaches and therefore should be able to read currents. The first rule (it bears repeating) is that higher wave action means stronger current. Currents take several forms. At a sandy beach with tiers of waves rolling in, current is visible in sections where the wave tiers are broken down and choppy. Surfers often ride this outbound river on their boards to get behind the sets. At coral reef shores—the best snorkeling spots—you can see current going out in blue channels and little rivers with rippled surfaces. Waves break over an offshore reef, water travels almost parallel to the shore in one direction or another, and escapes in a channel—a natural opening in the reef. Get caught in one of these babies and you're taking a ride.

How not to get caught in a rip current: Ask a lifeguard, if one is present. Always spend many minutes observing the waves and reading the current before entering. Don't assume the water is safe because you see tourists swimming. To test rip current, throw in a stick to see where it goes. Swimming with a buddy is a good idea, probably safest when the buddy is on shore watching and able to call for help (and also able to watch your stuff).

A mask and swim fins greatly enhance your swimming efficiency and power. Float face down periodically to see if you are being carried away. If there is a mild current, swim against it while you're snorkeling to be able to swim with it on the homeward leg. If you do get overpowered in a current, don't panic and don't tire yourself by swimming directly into the force. Breathe and stay calm. Wave for help. Swim sideways to an outgoing current, thereby getting out of the "river." Riptides and currents are near-shore phenomena, and they will release you offshore. You can then swim around the direction of the current to come back in. All of the above tips are trumped by the mantra for sea safety: "When in doubt, don't go out."

2. ROGUE WAVES

A rogue wave is a fairly rare gangsta' wave that arrives unexpectedly after many smaller sets have been rolling in. More commonplace big waves also nab people who get into poor position along the shore and underestimate the power of falling water. Wave heights vary each day without the apparent influence of other weather, and when a big one rolls in, terra firma turns into the rapids of a river.

How to not get bashed by a wave: Always keep an eye on the ocean when you are walking a coastline. Waves move fairly slowly and if you see a big one looming you can outrun it. The most dangerous spots on the shore are where the reef is already wet, and along sloping, soft sand at the receding foam line. The most powerful of swimmers have no chance against a rogue wave. At less threatening shorelines (flatter sand, small waves) stay within a quick dash of children.

How not to fall off a cliff or have one fall on you: Stay on the trail and back from precipices. Greenery disguises drop-offs on most tropical ridge trails. If hiking with kids, make sure to keep them under wraps. Don't step off the trail to take a picture without carefully checking the ground stability. A retractable hiking pole is useful, both to probe greenery and to thwart an unexpected gravity ride, a la using an ice ax to thwart a slide on snow. Stay off eroded faces and don't dally under cliffs. In dangerous areas, look up as you go, particularly on windy days when your ears won't give fair warning. The falling-rock hazard increases during and after rains, and especially on trails leading up narrow streambeds—and under waterfalls. Also remember that trails become slick after rains and their surfaces are usually rooted and rocky: missteps are likely unless you pay attention.

Watermen reunite a couple at Anini Beach, Kauai

3. FALLING OFF A CLIFF OR HAVING ONE FALL ON YOU

Geology happens in real time in Hawaii. Erosion is continual. The ground cannot be relied upon to be stable. Mountain and ridge faces are near vertical, held in check by tangles of flora. Trails often skirt these edges. Even techie-climbers with the talc and fancy shoes can screw up on easy ascents. Rocks are like large peanuts stuck in chocolate.

4. GETTING SWEPT AWAY

In Hawaii, yearly rain can be measured in feet—with tropical mountains on Maui, Oahu, and the Big Island getting 20-to-30 feet, and Kaua'i's Mount Waialeale drenched with more than 40 feet, the wettest spot on earth. Only a thick mat of flora prevents the islands from becoming a brown stain on the ocean. The steep and fissured topography is able to release millions of gallons into the sea via streams that rapidly rise

How Not To Have A Killer Vacation, cont'd—

to torrents. Often, mauka (mountain) showers will be taking place, while nearer the coast the day is bright and sunny. When auto incidents are included with hiking mishaps, flash floods are Hawaii's most lethal weather phenomenon.

How not to be swept away: During rains, avoid trails in gulches and narrow streambeds. Do not cross streams during high water. When you feel it is safe to cross, bear in mind that bedrock can be slippery. A hiking pole aids in stability, as does crossing in pairs with the stronger person downstream. If you get caught on the wrong side of a raging stream, wait it out. It will subside. When in narrow streambeds, you will hear a flash flood coming: get to high ground like now. What does it sound like? You'll know.

5. GETTING SWALLOWED BY THE LAND

At popular mainland parks, hikers are advised to stay on trails to avoid destroying a fragile ecosystem. In Hawaii, the tables are turned and the smart money is on the flora. Dense snarls of greenery make it impossible to find your way back to a trail after straying only a short distance. Throw in a little rain or fog, and you can become rapidly, hopelessly lost. To complete the horror show, add the hidden promise of earth cracks and lava tubes.

Kahaulea Rain Forest, Big Island

How not to get swallowed by the land: Stay on the trail. People have been walking these islands for centuries, and if there isn't already a trail, forget about getting there. If you lose a trail, backtrack to a known point. If the trail becomes hard to follow, you're not on a trail. Many trails are not signed or poorly marked, although some will be marked with plastic ribbon. As you proceed, look back occasionally to memorize the return route. Also memorize junctions, where you can leave a marker arrow with sticks—though remember to scatter the marker upon your return. Note your departure time on a hike, and make sure to begin your return when you have used up less than half the remaining daylight.

Even fit hikers will be lucky to make two miles an hour on Hawaiian trails, which often squiggle in all directions, have poor footing, and offer many reasons to take a scenic pause. If you do get caught out at night without a flashlight, stay put. If hiking in groups, stay together.

FREE ADVICE & OPINION

Factoids that will take some of the hassle and mystery out of a Hawaiian vacation.

BEACHES ACCESS

All beaches in Hawaii are public, regardless of private ownership of the land along the coast. That doesn't mean you can cut through someone's dining room to get to the surf. But virtually every beach has "Beach Access" or "Shoreline Public Access," or a similarly designated right-of-way. Sometimes parking near these access points can be a problem and occasionally you need to hike a trail or rock-hop a short coastal section to get to the beach. Signage can be obscure or nonexistent at some beaches, which adds to a sense of adventure. Exception: Military bases, a few on Oahu and one on the northwest shore of Kaua'i do not allow visitors, except for military personnel and their families.

At luxury resorts, beach access may be controlled, with a limited number of parking spaces that may be monitored by an entrance station. Several South Kohala resorts on the Big Island and one or two on Oahu have controlled entry. Ask for a beach access permit. When beach parking is full, visitors may request a pass to visit the resort for shopping or dining. Visitors usually are not monitored after entering resort grounds.

At public beach parks, Hawaiians gather on weekends for outdoor grilling and parties. First-year birthdays are big. Tourists are welcomed at beach parks, but be aware that the beaches are neighborhoods for Hawaiians that go back generations and you are a guest. You will find locals to be surprisingly friendly to the well-intentioned visitor.

Most developed beach parks are county-operated and fairly well maintained. You can expect showers, restrooms, and picnic pavilions. A number of other developed facilities are part of state parks, and these more often will be run-down and poorly maintained. Perhaps there is a plan in place to clean up these parks, but it's moving slowly. Funding will be cited as a limit-

A safe spot at Ehukai Beach Park, Oahu

ing factor, if you care to ask. The spiffiest beach facilities will be at the beach access parking area of resorts, built as part of the trade-off for developing near the beach.

HIKING AND TRAIL ACCESS

Many trails in use today were established by the earliest Hawaiians. Whether along the coast or into the mountains, the topography allows only certain routes. Along the coast, particularly on the Big Island and Maui, significant segments of ancient trails remain. Cobblestones or flat rocks embedded in sharper rocks tell the tale.

Hiking and Trail Access, cont'd—

Unlike beaches, no overriding rule governs access to state forest reserves and other public lands inland from the coast. Today, the best-developed and signed trail systems are at national parks and monuments; Hawaii Volcanoes, Pu'uhonua O' Honaunau, and Pu'ukohola Heiau on the Big Island, and Haleakala on Maui.

Most inland trails are on state property, and the most well maintained and signed trails are part of the state's Na Ala Hele ("trails for walking") system, which publicizes its trails, posts trailhead signs, and erects mileage markers along the way. Trails within actual state parks are also fairly well signed, although mainland visitors will be surprised at the poor maintenance at many Hawaii State Parks. (Notable exceptions are the cared-for Kalopa and Manuka parks on the Big Island, He'eia State Park on Oahu, and Waianapanapa State Park on Maui.) A number of factors contribute to the condition of state parks, and many people are working to make things better.

Many if not most of state forest roads and trails are not part of Na Ala Hele or state parks, but rather forest reserves and natural areas. Access varies. Many of the roads into forest reserves are open to hikers and mountain bikes. Some are only open to hunters, for the purpose of plugging wild pigs and goats, which are rooting about and damaging watersheds. Hunting is even a popular weekend pursuit on Oahu, where sportsmen begin at the end of suburban cul de sacs at the base of the mountains. Hikers are allowed in most hunting areas, though bright clothing and weekday (non-hunting period) use is recommended. Some state forestlands prohibit hikers. Entry is often ambiguous.

Other hiking trails are partially on large parcels of private lands with no signs to indicate one way or the other. "Use your own judgment" is the catch phrase. This book does not contain legal advice, but readers should go under the assumption that landowners are not responsible for injuries suffered by someone using their land for recreational purposes.

ROADS AND DRIVING

Automobile accidents, statistically speaking, are the biggest threat to your pursuit of happiness in paradise. Only Oahu has freeways, but they are not the problem. Experienced commuters from suburban mainland will not be intimidated by the driving habits of freeway drivers—although incidences of youth-or-alcohol-enhanced road rage do occur. The perplexing aspects of Oahu's freeways are exits with no corresponding on-ramps, serpentine connector routes that are ambiguously signed, and logjams into and out of Honolulu, particularly a hellish, dozen-lane confluence of the island's three main freeways. But seriously, it's not bad if you have a map book and copilot. And Oahu's H-3 Freeway from the Windward Coast through the Ko'olau Mountains is maybe the most amazing freeway car ride in the United States—and that's saying something.

At the other end of the spectrum, the island's narrow roads don't create the accidents you'd expect, probably because drivers are white-knuckling the wheel with senses keened. Maui's Hana Highway is a well-known for its single lanes, but it is easier to navigate than the segment a few miles beyond Hana that connects with Nu'u Bay on the south coast, or the north Maui run through Kahulokoa Village. Kaua'i's north shore from Princeville to road's end at the Kalalau Trail also has some narrow lanes.

Tourism creates traffic in certain areas (see *Picking an Island Style*, page 48). Other traffic is more prosaic. On many Hawaiian highways, even outside of Oahu, you will be going too slowly to dent a car should you hit something. The jams occur around traditional commute times, when tourists and locals alike join to create a gridfest.

The heavy traffic on Maui occurs going into and out of Kihei on the south leeward coast and Lahaina on the north leeward coast. Getting into Paia on the windward coast can be a hassle in the afternoon. On the Big Island, traffic gets backed up for several miles north of Kona in the afternoons and can proceed at jogging speed for

20 miles to Captain Cook. Drive times have been quadrupled over the last decade. Kaua'i's slow trap takes place mainly from Wailua through Kapa'a, over six or eight miles, since they have used a "contra-flow" lane system that relieves traffic where it's needed in the mornings and evening between the Lihue and Kapa'a. On the other side of Lihue, toward Poipu, traffic backs up for several miles headed into and through Lihue in the afternoons. City planners have noted these backups and are studying a possible relationship between real estate development and traffic.

Most tourist-related accidents happen on the pretty two-lane highways. The Mamalahoa, or Belt Highway, on the Big Island is of particular concern. It contours the island for a large segment above the coast, has no shoulder in many places, and is frequented by maniacs trying to shave a few minutes off the run from Hilo to Kona. Few other island highways present an inherent hazard—if you handle them correctly.

Surfmobile, Haleiwa, Oahu

Driving Tips

The car reaching a one-lane bridge first has the right of way ... Stop and allow that car and the ones behind it to proceed ... Cars stopped and lined up to cross the bridge may go once oncoming traffic has passed ... Don't speed up to catch a line of cars already on the bridge ... Stop and wait for oncoming traffic ... On the Hana Highway and other narrow scenic roads, pull over and let faster traffic go ahead ... Locals have places to be ...

Drive it or park it: don't slow down and look at scenery ... Pull safely off the roadway when you stop ... Have a copilot to give directions and spot for traffic when entering busier highways and roads ... Watch out for careless cars: people are gawking at scenery ... Car karma: allow turns and merges, and don't ride someone's bumper ... Drive aloha ... Watch out for drunks, especially at dusk on weekends ... And of course at closing time ...

Never leave valuables in the car ... Especially on Oahu, the most likely place in the nation to have a car break-in ... Even more than bear break-ins in Yosemite

... Don't transfer stuff to the trunk in the parking lot ... Thieves often work in pairs, and often it's boy-girl ... Broken glass in the parking lot is a sign of prior break-ins ... Thieves normally break into tourist cars, rather than locals' (except on Oahu, where everyone joins in the fun) ... Hang a necklace or beads from your rearview mirror to give your car a local look ... Or put a local bumper sticker in the back window ... Maps on the seats say, "I'm a tourist" ... So do hotel parking permits ... Leave a note on the dash reading "No Valuables" ... The odds are very unlikely that you will have a car break-in while on vacation ....

Make sure to have water and food along for the ride ... When everyone is staring blankly or becoming testy, it's time stop the car, get out, and have some beverages and snacks .... Baby wipes (packaged, moistened towelettes) are a good way to tidy up before and after a picnic ... Rental car companies can charge a cleaning fee, so don't thrash it ... Watch out for pedestrians and cyclists ... Be prepared for Nene Crossings, Banana Virus Areas, and Donkey Zones ... And, seriously, don't drive across a spillway or road that is covered by water higher than the bottom of your rims.

PART FOUR
The Best Of Hawaii

Blue Lagoon, Big Island

What do you want to do on your Hawaiian vacation?
The various answers to that question are listed below
in the 36 BEST OF categories.

Within each category, Hawaii's top 20 (maximum) places
are listed. Each island will have its share, depending on its
strength in that category. The listings aren't prioritized one
through 20, but rather grouped as the top 20—except that the
Best of the Best (usually five) will be **boldfaced**. Each island
may or may not have a boldfaced listing.

Worth a Look listings are just that, and many might make
someone's top 20. A long list of Worth-a-Looks also indicates a
strong suit for an island in that category.

AND THE WINNER IS ... the island with the most *Best Of*
listings for a particular category. Sometimes the winner will
be obvious. For some categories, where all islands are strong,
picking a winner is a close call or a tie, resulting in co-winners
for that category.

A Word of Heresy: After visiting all the places in the *Best Of*
listings, you could well conclude that there is no absolute
"best" of anything. Instead, you may find some anonymous
nook in the wilds or a detail in an obscure museum that brings
on a personal epiphany. Or, you may hit one of the great places
on a dreary day or in time to stand next to some dweeb
cell-phoning his divorce attorney, creating an aura of
unpleasantness. And, your favorite spot might be someone
else's ho-hum.

In short, there is no accounting for personal tastes and
serendipity.

THE BEST OF HAWAII *Scorecard*
A summary of category winners.

Category & Page Number	Kauai	Oahu	Maui	Big Island
1. BEGINNER SNORKELING, page 68			×	
2. OVERALL GOOD SNORKELING, page 69				×
3. QUEEN'S BATHS, KEIKI (KIDS') BEACHES, page 72				×
4. FAMILY DAY AT THE BEACH, page 74			×	
5. A BOOK, A BEACH AND THEE, page 76	×			
6. BABE & HUNK BEACHES, page 78		×		
7. COASTAL BLUFFS, TIDE POOLS, BIG WAVES, page 79				×
8. HIKE-TO WILD BEACHES, page 81	×			
9. DRIVE-UP SCENIC BEACH HIKES, page 83	×			
10. WHALES & WILDLIFE, page 84	×		×	×
11. WAVES FOR THE BIG BOYS, page 86		×		
12. RELIABLE SPOTS FOR GOOD SURFERS, page 87		×		
13. LEARN-TO-SURF BEACHES, page 89		×		
14. BODYBOARDING, page 89		×		
15. BEST PLACES TO WATCH SURFERS, page 91		×		
16. WINDSURFING & KITE-BOARDING, page 92			×	
17. KAYAKING: RIVER LAGOONS & OCEAN, page 93	×		×	
18. MUSEUMS & GALLERIES, page 95		×		
19. ATTRACTIONS & VISITOR CENTERS, page 97		×		
20. HAWAIIAN TEMPLES & ANCIENT SITES, page 100				×
21. BOTANICAL GARDENS, page 103	×			
22. WALK-AROUND TOURIST TOWNS, page 105		×		
23. SWANK RESORTS, page 108			×	×
24. INSPIRING CHURCHES & HOLY PLACES, page 110			×	
25. SCENIC DRIVES, page 112	×			×
26. PICNIC PARKS, page 114			×	×
27. TROPICAL RIDGE & PEAK HIKES, page 116	×			
28. WATERFALLS, page 118			×	
29. RAIN FOREST & STREAM VALLEY HIKES, page 120				×
30. EASY WALKS TO CLASSIC HAWAIIAN VISTAS, page 122	×			
31. DRY AND HIGH HIKES, page 124			×	
32. BIRDWATCHING FOREST HIKES, page 126	×			
33. VOLCANO CRATERS & LAVA HIKES, page 128				×
34. BICYCLE TOURING & MOUNTAIN BIKING, page 130	×			×
35. HORSEBACK RIDING, page 132	×		×	×
36. GOLF, page 134			×	

Pokai Beach Park, Oahu; Wailea, Maui, Mauna Lani Resort fishponds, Big Island

1. BEGINNER SNORKELING
Easiest-entry, fish-filled calm waters to get you hooked on snorkeling

KAUA'I
BEACH HOUSE BEACH
Dreary curbside appeal belies the coral heads, fish, and turtles. Near Prince Kuhio Park, it's among Kaua'i's best.

POIPU BEACH
Easy sandy entry at the beach park. Not tons of fish.

Worth a Look: LYDGATE PARK (WAILUA)

OAHU
HANAUMA BAY NATURE PRESERVE
Looks dreamy from above, but crowds and drab coral keep it a notch from the top.

MAGIC ISLAND
Man-made pool at Ala Moana Park.

MAUI
KAMAOLE BEACH PARKS
The rocky tips between the three beach parks in Kihei are home to fish and coral. Nice sandy entries and not overcrowded.

LA PEROUSE BAY-AHIHI COVE
Pristine waters off the jagged shore of Maui's most recent volcanic eruption.

ULUA-MOKAPU BEACHES
Nice sandy nooks in front of Wailea's resorts with easy entry and near-shore coral.

BIG ISLAND
KAHALU'U BEACH PARK
Kona's beach park is protected by a reef and supports acres of fish-filled coral. The parking lot fills up early.

BEACH CLUB BEACH
Fewer swimmers know the charms of this baby, located at the south end of the beaches at Mauna Lani Resort.

CARLSMITH BEACH PARK
If the sun appeared more often, this county beach park with a huge man-made pool would score even higher.

AND THE WINNER IS ... All the islands have choices, but MAUI edges the Big Island for the best snorkeling for beginners.

Windward Oahu, near Makai Research Pier

2. OVERALL GOOD SNORKELING
The best spots for intermediate to advanced snorkelers.

KAUA'I

TUNNELS
Coral boils down into a blue channel, off a sandy beach, rimmed by jagged "Bali Hai" mountain. Parking is problematic; show up early or late.

KE'E BEACH
At the Kalalau Trailhead, Ke'e gets hammered with footsteps on nice days. But this big sandy-bottomed oval beneath Napali (The Cliffs) is worth the hassle.

LEHUA ISLAND
You'll need to hop a charter in Port Allen and cruise 20 miles to the gin-clear water of this little bird sanctuary next to Ni'ihau.

Worth a Look: HIDEAWAYS-KENOMENE BEACH (Princeville); ANINI BEACH, AHUKINI LANDING (Lihue Airport), WHALER'S COVE (Poipu-Kuhio), HOUSE BEACH (Anahola)

OAHU

MAKAI RESEARCH PIER
Tour companies van people to this easy-entry coral garden on the Windward Side. You swim around near the pilings of the dock house for the little subs used by the University of Hawaii.

THREE TABLES-SHARK'S COVE
Close-together "snorkeling parks" on the North Shore, in Pupukea. Usually summer only. Lot's of interesting formations.

CROMWELL'S COVE
A sense of place: beautiful cove at Black Point, near the ritzy mansion of Shangri-la. The fab place was the 1937 vision of heiress Doris Duke, queen of the arts.

Worth a Look: LANIKAI BEACH (Kailua); GOAT ISLAND (Windward-north), KAHE POINT (West Side), KAIONA BEACH PARK (Waimanalo), KALUAHOLE BEACH (Diamond Head), ALLIGATOR ROCK (North Shore), and MOKOLI'I ISLAND (Chinaman's Hat-Windward)

MAUI

HONOLUA MARINE PRESERVE
After walking down the highway from a parking lot, crossing a stream under a giant banyan, and and arriving at a rocky beach, you may have doubts. Then get in the water and go flying over fish-rich coral hillocks.

CHANG'S POINT-TURTLE TOWN
Entry can be chancy from the lava spit, but not bad. Tour boats anchor within 200 feet of shore. Yes, there are turtles.

MOLOKINI ISLAND
Join the crew of the flotilla of boats that take the short cruise to the volcanic crescent island three miles offshore Kihei. Visibility and marine life are right up there with the best in Hawaii.

KALAELOA COVE (AQUARIUM)
All that a'a lava (the sharp kind) on shore translates to very clear water. Lots of people, occasionally too many, make the pesky half-mile hike.

OLOWALU BEACH
Roadside parking and easy sand entry not far south of Lahaina. You'll have company, including snorkel tours that anchor here. A good option for families.

CORAL GARDENS
Experienced snorkelers will want to make the swim to this cove, located at the Lahaina side of the highway tunnel. Check it out from the guardrail above. You may see tour boats anchored.

NU'U LANDING
For adventure snorkelers, this is a find on calmer days. Nu'u is on the isolated south shore. A short walk leads to tiny clear pockets in a low, lava point. Could be the next big thing.

Worth a Look: PU'UNOA BEACH (Lahaina), ONEULI (Black Sand) BEACH (Makena), WAIANAPANAPA STATE PARK (Hana), KAPALUA BAY, BLACK ROCK-SHERATON BEACH (Ka'anapali), WASH ROCK (McGregor Point), HALEKI'I BAY (Kaupo)

Tunnels, Kauai

Overall Good Snorkeling, cont'd—

BIG ISLAND

TWO STEP
Tabletop sections of a smooth-lava reef provide entry for the best easy-access snorkeling in Hawaii. Next to Pu'uhonua O Honaunau National Park.

CAPTAIN COOK MONUMENT
Kayak, sail, or hike down 1,300 feet to get to this historic spot at the north mouth of Kealakekua Bay—which draws crowds. A wall of coral lines a near-shore drop-off.

WAIOPAE TIDE POOLS MARINE DISTRICT
A marine conservation district on the north Puna Coast is the site of numerous, large tide pools rich in sea life. Otherworldly.

MAHUKONA WHARF
Step down a ladder at the wharf of an old sugar mill in Kohala. Ship wreckage adds interest to the snorkel, as do the occasional harmless ray and octopus.

KAWAI POINT
Experienced flipper fiends can shore-dive where tour boats anchor, from the north end of Kona's Old Airport Beach.

FROG ROCK-KOHALA WATERFRONT
Only high swells detract from these out-of-the-way snorkeling venues at the south end of the Kohala coast. Not for novices.

KEALAKEKUA HISTORICAL PARK
Pick a day when the bodyboarders aren't there (lower surf) and you'll find excellent conditions for the coral hills to the left side of the rocky beach.

Worth a Look: BEACH 69 (Waialea Bay-Hapuna) HONOMALINO BEACH (Miloli'i), KEAHOU SUNDECK (near Sheraton), KAHUWAI BAY (Kona Village); NINOLE COVE (Black Sands-Pahala), MOKU OLA (Coconut Island-Hilo), KEAWAIKI BAY-BROWN'S RETREAT (South Kohala), KOAI'E COVE (Lapakahi State Park), MAKAHA CAVERNS (Makaha)

AND THE WINNER IS ... Give the edge to the BIG ISLAND in a slugfest with Maui. With no stream runoff, the Big Island's near-shore waters sparkle. Maui has many accessible, easy-entry spots that are not as far apart. Oahu and Kaua'i tie for third and will deliver the goods—just not in as many places.

Puunoa Beach, Maui

3. QUEEN'S BATHS, FRESH POOLS, KEIKI (KIDS') BEACHES
Queens baths (tide pools) make great pools, when surf is low. Slack rivers provide fresh water swimming opportunities. Reefs form pools, perfect for toddlers and dawdlers.

KAUA'I

QUEEN EMMAS BATHS
A steep trail down from a Princeville neighborhood leads to a tidal shelf with several pools. High surf can be a hazard.

LUMAHAI RIVER POOL
In dry weather, a sand dam blocks the river flow at this scenic beach, creating a clear-green swimming lagoon.

WATERHOUSE BEACH
Tucked away in a neighborhood at Whaler's Cove, near Poipu.

QUEENS POND POLIHALE
A near-shore reef creates a swimming oval along the miles-long Barking Sands Beach. Bring shade, and avoid at high surf.

Worth a Look: KIPU FALLS POOL (Puhi), KALIHIWAI STREAM POOL (Kilauea), KAPA'A BABY BEACH, KOHOLALELE (Secret) FALLS POOL (Wailua River)

OAHU

KAIHALULU BEACH KEIKI POND
Head a half-mile up the sand from Turtle Bay Resort on the North Shore to find a perfect pond at an opening in the reef.

LANIKUHONUA COVE
Next to man-made Ko Olina Resort lagoons is nature's better effort, on the grounds of Lanikuhonua Hawaiian Cultural Park.

MOTHERS BEACH
Kahala Beach, with numerous public access spots, is in a ritzy neighborhood, just around the corner of Diamond Head from Waikiki.

Worth a Look: MAUNAWILI FALLS POOL (Windward), KAENA KEIKI POND (Yokohama Bay), MAKAPU'U TIDE POOLS , WAIMANO FALLS POOLS (Pearl City), KAHANA STREAM SWIMMING HOLE (Windward)

MAUI

BABY BALDWIN BEACH
At the far end of Baldwin Beach Park is one of Hawaii's best keiki beaches—a good vibe, and a big reef-protected oval.

POOLS OF OHEO
The pools and cascades at this lower section of Haleakala National Park is the terminus for many Hana Highway tourists. Can be a zoo in nice weather and dangerous during rains.

BELLSTONE POOL (OLIVINE POOL)
North shore tide pool before Kahukola Village is a walk down from the highway. Sweet, but watch for waves.

BLUE POOL
Off the highway before getting to Hana, this oceanside fresh pool sits beneath ribonny Blue Angel Falls. Popularity has soured some of the locals.

KEANAE (SAPPHIRE) POOLS
A short scramble down from a bend in Hana Highway leads to this beauty. Farther down stream, at the ocean, is a huge river pool.

Worth a Look: WAIANAPANAPA CAVES (Hana), TWIN FALLS (Hana Highway), VENUS POOL (past Hana, access issues), KOIEIE LOKO IA FISHPOND (North Kihei), HONOKOWAI BEACH PARK (South Kapalua)

Two Step, Big Island

BIG ISLAND

KAPOHO SEAPOOL (CHAMPAGNE COVE)

A fantastic quirk of nature tucked into rugged
Cape Kumukahi on the nose of the sunny
Puna Coast. Immerse yourself in sparkling
clear, not too hot, not too cold.

MAKALAWENA KEIKI BEACH

It's a bit of a hike from Kona's Kekaha Kai
State Park to this jewel of a beachside pool.
Parklike trees add to the effect. Easy trail
across lava—if you bring hats and water.

BOILING POTS-RAINBOW FALLS POOLS

Providing it hasn't rained, these pools near
falls at Hilo's Wailuku River State Park are
Hawaii's best freshwater dips.

MAUA LANI QUEENS BATH

Wander the margins of the resort's large
fishponds to find this man-made soaking tub.

RIVIERA POOL

Man-made shoreside tub behind the Kona By
the Sea condos, in the middle of the Kailua
strip. Low tide makes it unappealing.

KE'EI SEAPOOL

Drive a bumpy road to Ke'ei Village, then walk
a mile around smooth-lava Palemanu Point to
find this underrated, man-enhanced tide pool.

AHALANUI HOT POND

A big warm man-made pool at ocean's edge,
under palms in a free county park. What's the
downside?

Worth a Look: OLD AIRPORT BEACH KEIKI
BEACH (Kailua-Kona), WAWAIOLI KEIKI POND
(just north of Kona), POHOIKI WARM SPRING
(Isaac Hale Beach Park, Puna), PU'UHONUA
KEIKI POND (beach park at the national park),
AIOPIO FISHTRAP (Kaloko Historic Park),
KIKAUA POINT PARK (South Kohala)

Mauna Lani Queens Bath, Big Island

AND THE WINNER IS ... The BIG ISLAND
kicks butt, though the other islands have
plenty of safe spots for small kids. Maui's
well-known pools have access concerns,
and are often crowded.

Baby Baldwin Beach, Maui

4. FAMILY DAY AT THE BEACH
Jump in the car with the kids and beach gear and spread out for a day of fun in the surf, sand, and sun.

KAUA'I
LYDGATE PARK
A large man-made ocean pool is the drawing card for Wailua's popular park. Pluses include picnic pavilions, playsets, historic sites, and lots of lawn.

HANALEI CITY PAVILION
Beach park in the middle of Hanalei Bay has a lawn and tables and safe swimming. Prime sand-castle territory.

POIPU BEACH
Next to the resorts on the sunny south, Poipu draws both tourists and locals. Pavilions and shaded tables.

ANINI BEACH
Two miles of reef near Princeville protect a quiet, nicely treed park, with pavilions and a polo field across the sleepy road.

SALT POND BEACH PARK
A sure thing on the sunny west side, at Hanapepe. Protected, large swimming area. Palms and picnic tables dot a big lawn.

Worth a Look: KALIHIWAI BEACH PARK (Kilauea), PONO KAI BEACH (Kapa'a)

OAHU
KAILUA BEACH PARK
Rolling lawn of the backshore breaks up a long stretch of sand. Kayaking to close-in Flat Island adds a fun option.

KAHANAMOKU BEACH PARK
A shaded little park pocketed into Waikiki, next to the Hilton Hawaiian Village. Safe swimming and not as crowded.

SECRET ISLAND-KUALOA REGIONAL PARK
Mokoli'i Island (Chinaman's Hat) is the signature feature, but take a walk inland on the curving shore to a scenic sand patch next to a historic fishpond (hiking tours do).

HALEIWA ALI'I BEACH PARK
TV's *Baywatch* was filmed here. A lot going on: surfing, boat harbor, snorkeling, canoeing, and a large lawn for running around.

Worth a Look: WHITE PLAINS BEACH PARK (Ewa), KO OLINA LAGOONS

Three Tables, Oahu; Kamaole Beach Park, Maui

MAUI

KAMAOLE BEACH PARKS
Take your pick among Kihei's three popular offerings. Good sand, safe swimming, lawns, facilities, and picnic tables.

PU'UNOA BEACH
Lahaina's Baby Beach. A reef protects the shore and provides for safe swimming among coral heads. Neighbor islands highlight the offshore view. No facilities.

KEAWAKAPU BEACH
Long sand strip between Kihei and the Wailua beaches.

MAKENA STATE PARK
Several large parking lots fill up, but there's always room on the sand at Big Beach—Maui's most wildly scenic.

KAPALUA BEACH
It may not be "America's Best Beach," as travel mags claims, but it is a fetching curve of sand with good swimming. In the middle of a resort area.

HAMOA BEACH
This beach, used by guests of Hotel Hana Maui (a few miles away), is the best bet for miles around on the south coast.

Worth a Look: KAHEKILI BEACH (Ka'anapali), NAPILI BEACH (Kapalua)

BIG ISLAND

MAUNA LANI-FAIRMONT RESORTS BEACHES
Nanku Inlet, Pauoa Bay, and Beach Club Beach offer families superlative choices at this serene resort strip with a gardenscaped backshore.

MAUNA KEA BEACH
The resort took a hit in the quake of 2006, but its classic crescent beach remains one of the best. Nice facilities, coastal path, and treed shoreline.

ONEKAHAKAHA BEACH PARK
Live like a Hawaiian. A huge man-made swimming oval, picnic pavilions, good facilities make this the best family park among Hilo's underrated offerings.

HAPUNA BEACH STATE PARK
When the state gets its act together with maintenance, this South Kohala favorite can head the list again.

Worth a Look: CARLSMITH BEACH PARK (Hilo); RICHARDSON OCEAN PARK (Hilo), KUA BAY (South Kohala)

AND THE WINNER IS ... MAUI has the most choices for families seeking surf, sun, and sand. All the other islands can lay claim to second.

Kamaole Beach Park, Maui

5. A BOOK, A BEACH, AND THEE
Couples seeking privacy can find a sunny spot to spend a quiet day, taking dips or retreating to shade to keep cool. These beaches are off the tourist track.

KAUA'I
LARSENS BEACH
A short hike down from pasturelands leads to more than a mile of wild beach. Monk seals and shorebirds like the rough lava-and-coral reef, and backshore flora.

WAIAKALUA BEACH
A hike-to-only special near Kilauea. The first beach is easy, and several other secluded beaches are reachable by rock-hopping the shore.

PAPA'A BAY
The estate of a Hollywood producer lies well back from the beach, but everyone else has to make a short walk to this blue crescent.

HANAPAI BEACH
A quarter-mile long stretch of sand and beach trees is 'hidden' to the right as the road makes a sweeping left toward Anini Beach Park.

MAHAULEPU
A few miles of bumpy road from the Grand Hyatt in Poipu leads to this beach. Great swimming. A coastal trail toward Hoary Head Ridge provides a getaway from this getaway.

KEPUHI BEACH
You can always find quietude, even when the crowds are pounding Tunnels and Ke'e beaches, which are just down the road.

WAIKOKO BEACH
The north end of Hanalei Bay has some lonesome sand and great mountain views—especially if you take the surfer's trail and not the roadside turnout.

Worth a Look: MOLOA'A BAY, ALIOMANU BAY

OAHU
KAWELA BEACH
Until the nearby Turtle Bay Resort achieves its grandiose expansion plans, this North Shore cove remains a sublime spot for a beach day.

KA'ALAWAI BEACH
Finding and parking near this beach near the Shangri La mansion at Black Point (below Diamond Head) isn't that easy. That's why it remains such a find.

MALAEKAHANA STATE RECREATION AREA
A huge, forest peninsula, rimmed by a sandy beach, points at Goat Island—which beckons adventure snorkelers.

MAKALEHA BEACH
Say hi to horses on a short walk though pastures to this beach that is one of the settings for Lost, the television program. Not far from Haleiwa on the Mokuleia Coast.

Worth a Look: ETERNITY BEACH (Halona Blow Hole), LAUMILO ACCESS-WAIMANALO BEACH (Windward), MAKALEI BEACH PARK (near Kapiolani Park)

MAUI
PO'OLENALENA BEACH
New, big homes have risen in the backshore, but two little beaches near Wailea remain relatively serene—due to many other choices in the vicinity.

WINDMILL BEACH
One of the few undeveloped beaches on Maui, north of Kapalua on the way to Honolua Bay.

Worth a Look: MALUAKA BEACH (Makena), SPRECKELSVILLE BEACH-SUGAR COVE, ONELOA BEACH (Kapalua)

BIG ISLAND
MAKALAWENA BEACH
A horrendous road and a hot, 45-minute hike thin the visitors to this beautiful run of dunes and trees. One of several Kekaha Kai State Park beaches.

HONOMALINO BEACH
Take a 20-minute walk from the village of Miloli'i, south of Kona, and you reach a crescent beach with palms.

BEACH 69 (WAIALEA BAY)
The word is out on this once secret beach next to Hapuna—the state has added a real parking lot, a few tables, and restrooms. But you can still find a private spot.

KAPALAOA BEACH
Head south on the sand from the popular beach park at Anaeho'omalu Bay (near the Hilton) to find sand suitable for snorkelers, turtles, and the occasional kite-boarder.

Worth a Look: KEHENA BLACK SAND (19-Mile) BEACH (Puna), ALULA BEACH (Honokohau Harbor), MAU'UMAE BEACH (Spencer Beach Park-Mauna Lani)

AND THE WINNER IS ... KAUA'I has the market cornered for kick-back beaches for couples. The Big Island has some good ones, but not as many. Oahu's sandy shores offer quietude in places.

Kekaha Kai State Park, Big Island

6. BABE & HUNK BEACHES

Check out the be-seen scene and stake out some sand of your own.

Waikiki, Oahu

KAUA'I

HANALEI BAY

Start at Black Pot Beach and Hanalei Pier and walk-jog the curving mile of flat sand, passing surfers and sunbathers, beach cottages and parks. A towering green ridge mirrors the bay's curve and all is right with the world.

POIPU BEACH-SHIPWRECK

A resort strip and beach park draw both tourists and locals along Kaua'i's scorched sand. Surfing, snorkeling, and beachside bars.

Worth an ogle: KEALIA BEACH (Kapa'a), KALAPAKI BEACH (Nawiliwili)

OAHU

PIPELINE

A big-wave day or competition make Pipe the place to be for the surf set. A shaded path beside Ehukai Beach Park at the backshore promotes mingling.

LANIKAI BEACH

Laid-back locals and independent tourists find their way to the glam beach on the Windward Side. Offshore islands, powder sand, and turquoise waters set the scene. Commercials and swimsuit catalogues are shot here.

KAPIOLANI PARK BEACHES

The huge grassy park at the Diamond Head end of Waikiki is the backdrop for Honolulu's metro set and tourists who want to walk.

WAIKIKI BEACH

How can you exclude this world famous beach? Acres of flesh that have seldom seen daylight are counterpoint to Waikiki's sex appeal.

SANDY BEACH

This hot bodyboarding beach rocks with highschoolers and up, the parking lot jammed with car stereos syncopating with the surf.

WAIMEA BAY

Pro surf scene amps the normal gathering.

Check it out: SUNSET BEACH (North Shore), WHITE PLAINS BEACH Park (Ewa)

MAUI

LAHAINA BEACHES

Beaches on either end of town bookend an LA-style beach scene. Touristy, yes, but locals also filter in from the beach-cottage neighborhoods.

KA'ANAPALI BEACH

Dubbed Dig Me Beach in the 1970s, Ka'anapali might be behind the cool curve, but it remains high on the hangout list. Start at the Hanako'o Beach Park and parade along the resort path past the Hyatt to the Sheraton.

HO'OKIPA BEACH

Just outside of hemp-hip Paia, this beach draws the big-time windsurfing and surf scene. Tourists gather at a viewing overlook while the locals carouse the parking lot below.

KANAHA BEACH PARK

Not a sunblock- and lounge-chair place, but windsurfers and kite-boarders make this a be-there beach. Hidden near the airport, Kanaha is missed by tourists. A view across the bay at Iao Valley adds to the aesthetic.

Scope the scene: KAMAOLE BEACH PARKS (Kihei); WAILEA RESORTS beach, LITTLE BEACH

BIG ISLAND

HAPUNA BEACH STATE PARK

The Big Island is not your spring break destination. Hapuna brings in a mass of local surfers and tourists—it's the sure-thing sun beach for refugees from east Hawaii.

AND THE WINNER IS ... If you're looking for glamorous singles beaches, OAHU is the pick. Maui is runner-up, and has an argument to be tops.

7. COASTAL BLUFFS, TIDE POOLS, BIG WAVES CRASH
Trails in the salt spray of dramatic seascapes and spots to watch explosions of white water.

KAUA'I

KEPUHI POINT-LARSENS
Seabirds and whales accent the landscape of this wave-tortured point on the northeast coast. A beachcomber's paradise.

MAHAULEPU HERITAGE TRAIL
Bluff leads from the Hyatt along a wild coast, passing Waiopili Heiau and tide pools.

QUEEN EMMAS BATHS
Watch the north coast's big ones roll in and take on the tidal shelf. Gets big winter surf.

Worth a look: KEALIA BEACH TO HOUSE BEACH

OAHU

YOKOHAMA BAY TO KAENA POINT
Hard to believe that a narrow-gauge railroad went around this point. Waves have obliterated key sections.

KA IWI SCENIC SHORELINE
Swimmable tide pools and an odd formation known as Pele's Rock add interest to the island's most easterly point.

MOKULEIA COAST TO KAENA POINT
On the other side of the Waianae Range from the Yokohama hike. This north coast has more tide pools.

MAUI

NAKALELE BLOWHOLE-OHAI LOOP TRAIL
A sea geyser, swirls of weird rock colorations, and a new nature trail: don't forget to keep a seaward eye peeled for waves and whales.

WAIANAPANAPA STATE PARK
Sharp lava and a series of ruins border a historic coastal trail near Hana. Beach flora softens the edges.

DRAGONS TEETH (MAKALUAPUNA POINT)
A fun walk out from the Ritz Carlton past jagged rocks, ending at a low point.

LIPOA POINT
This wave-watchers roost (at Honolua Bay) is off the radar screen for most tourists.

Worth a Look: HAWEA POINT SHORELINE CONSERVATION AREA (Kapalua), SEABIRD BLUFFS (Windward), MANAWAINUI GULCH-KING'S TRAIL (south coast)

Larsens Beach (on the way to Kepuhi Point), Kauai

Coastal Bluff Hiking, cont'd—

BIG ISLAND

WELIWELI POINT-KAWAI POINT
In 1859, a violent introduction took place as a stampede of Mauna Loa's lava met ocean waves. Coral heaps are mixed into the resulting sculpture.

KUAMO'O BATTLEFIELD
The 1819 intra-island war that took place here (to end the kapu system) is long over, but the sea rages on. A safe nook in a protruding rock gives you the best ringside seat in Hawaii.

SOUTH POINT
The end-point of the 1,600-mile Hawaiian Archipelago is a dynamic spot to watch land versus sea.

KI'ILAE VILLAGE COASTAL TRAIL
Ruins beneath the Keane'e Cliffs highlight a historic trail from the Pu'uhonua O Honaunau National Park.

CAPE KUMUKAHI
Several acres of the jagged lava were added by a 1960 eruption. The large stacks, however, are the King's Pillar and they've been a landmark for mariners since the 1500s.

KOHANAIKI COASTAL PARK
Take a seashell hunt amid the coral drifts and beach flora on the way to one of Kona's best surfing spots, Pinetrees.

DONKEY TRAIL TO ONOMEA BAY
The lush Hawaii Tropical Botanical Gardens reside above this seascape. One point is like walking the plank—only safer.

LAUPAHOEHOE POINT BEACH PARK
The tragic tidal wave that took out a school here in 1946 did little damage to the lava stacks.

Worth a Look: LIGHTHOUSE BEACH (Kohala) KE-AHOU SURF BLOWHOLES, LEHIA BEACH PARK (Hilo), KEALIA BEACH (Ho'okena Beach Park)

AND THE WINNER IS ... With many more miles of coast and fewer sandy beaches, the BIG ISLAND is the place to watch the land do battle with the sea. Beach-rich Maui also has rugged coast on both its northern and southern shores.

Blue Lagoon, Big Island

8. HIKE-TO WILD BEACHES
Unspoiled beaches reachable only by foot from inshore trailhead parking.

KAUA'I
SECRET BEACH
Okay, it's not a huge secret anymore. But you'll always find space on this mile-long run of sand—encased by cliffs that rim around to Kilauea Lighthouse.

DONKEY BEACH
Walk an old pineapple haul road, or take a trail through a new, gated community, down to a very large crescent of sand along miles of open coast. Surfers, sunbathers, and cyclists like it.

LARSENS BEACH
A classic getaway for beachcombers. A one-lane road through pasture gives way to a blue-water vista of the miles-long beach. Tide pools and reefs break up the shoreline.

HIDEAWAYS-KENOMENE BEACH
Surfing and snorkeling are down a flight of rickety steps, beginning near the tennis courts at the entrance to posh Princeville Resort.

WAIAKALUA BEACH-PILA'A BEACHES
These come as close to Gilligan's Island as you'll get in Hawaii. Coco palms and ironwoods grace several ample strips of sand. A little rock hopping is required to see all the beaches.

PAPA'A BAY
As you round the bluff on the short trail near Anahola, you will be coaxed down by a tree-filtered view of this cobalt bay and white-sand beach.

HAULA BEACH
Poipu's Mahaulepu coast ends at this pink-rock cove set below the high-rising Hoary Head Ridge.

HANAKAPIAI BEACH
A worthy destination for a 4-mile, round-trip hike on the Kalalau Trail. Winter surf is treacherous for swimming.

Worth a Look: RUNNING WATERS BEACH (Nawiliwili), SEA LODGE BEACH (Princeville)

OAHU
A couple of beaches (listed elsewhere) involve a short hike; but practically speaking, all of Oahu's beaches can be accessed by shoreline parking.

MAUI
RED SAND BEACH
A red cinder cone at sea level, protected by and eyebrow reef, this one wins the most-unusual beach award. The popular trail is iffy: one spot skirts a ledge and the access is via private property.

BEAU CHIEN BEACH
A short walk from road's end at lava-strewn La Perouse Bay, leads to a coral-rock shore at the start of the historic, cobblestone King's Trail.

BIG ISLAND
MAKALAWENA-MAHAIULA BAY
Three beach oases are the pot of gold at the end of a ridiculously bumpy road across lava at Kekaha Kai State Park—north of the Kona Airport.

HONOMALINO BEACH
South Kona's ace in the hole. A 20-minute walk from the village of Miloli'i gets you to a palm-studded crescent of sand. Dolphins like the little bay.

MAU'UMAE BEACH
An excellent swimming nook, replete with a variety of beach trees, halfway between Spencer Beach Park and the Mauna Kea Hotel.

KEAWAIKI BAY
The old Brown Estate, site of 1920s parties, is a sideshow after you walk the lava-wasteland trail to the coast. Great snorkeling and beachcombing along a wild coast.

BLUE LAGOON
The aquamarine streak at the edge of a palm oasis is visible from a lava-baked scenic vista at the highway. The lure is irresistible.

POLOLU BEACH
Head down to the valley at the end of the road in Kohala. The rough, driftwood-strewn beach and valley is the beginning of the Big Island's wilderness coast.

Worth a Look: WAIPIO BEACH, GREEN SAND BEACH (South Point), HONOKOHAU BEACH (Kaloko National Historic Park).

AND THE WINNER IS ... KAUA'I is the place to go to find those fantasy beaches on foot. The Big Island is a respectable runner-up.

Pololu Beach, Big Island; Honolua Bay near Lipoa Point, Maui; Lumahai Beach, Kauai; Makua Beach, Oahu

Makena State Beach (Big Beach), Maui

9. DRIVE-UP SCENIC BEACH HIKES
*Park at an undeveloped beach and hike a mile or more
along the sand and reefs of an unspoiled beach.*

KAUA'I
LUMAHAI BEACH
Man, this beauty looks like something out of
the movie *South Pacific*. Oh, that's right, it is.
Huge surf and tropical flora.

BARKING SANDS BEACH
A potholed road ends on arid west Kaua'i at
Polihale State Beach. Here, the Napali (Cliffs)
end, giving way to miles of wide sand—
Hawaii's longest at 11 miles (though some
of it is on an off-limits military base).

KAHILI BEACH
Among the island's wealth of wild beaches is
this one at Kilauea Bay. Featured is a jungle
stream abutting a wildlife refuge.

MAHAULEPU
Monk seals join humans on a mile-long run
from Gillians Beach to Kawailoa Bay.

KEPUHI POINT TO HAENA BEACH PARK
A north shore secret. Collect tiny seashells in
the yellow sand and walk pools in the onshore
reef.

ANAHOLA BAY-ALIOMANU
A narrow strip of sand skirts leafy beach trees
and modest cottages. Eastern exposure
collects treasure for beachcombers.

Worth a Look: **NU'UKOLI BEACH-LYDGATE PARK**
(Wailua), **PAKALA BEACHES** (Waimea), **KEKAHA
BEACH**

OAHU
HANAKAILIO BEACH
Park at Turtle Bay Resort and stomp the sand
past Kahuku Point (Oahu's most northerly) to
this isolated, wild beach.

WAIMANALO BEACH
Two big, forested parks bookend this
beachwalk. Rabbit Island beautifies the ocean
horizon, while the Ko'olau Range frames the
backshore.

MALAEKAHANA STATE RECREATION AREA
You can walk for several miles on a beach that
wraps the tip of a forested peninsula.

Drive-up Scenic Beach Hikes, cont'd—

MAKUA BEACH
This West Side beach and valley were a setting for the movie version of Michener's *Hawaii*

KUILEI CLIFFS TO SHANGRI LA MANSION
The cliffs and surfer's waves sandwich this narrow beach, isolated below Diamond Head.

Worth a Look: MOKULEIA BEACH PARK TO CAMP ERDMAN (North Shore), NIMITZ BEACH PARK TO WHITE PLAINS BEACH (Ewa), PIPELINE TO SUNSET BEACH (North Shore)

MAUI

MAKENA STATE PARK
Big Beach and Little Beach are undeveloped. Haleakala's green slopes rise at the backshore toward Ulupalakua Ranch.

MA'ALAEA BAY
Flat sand make this bay, on the west side of Maui's isthmus, a favorite for joggers

Worth a Look: SPRECKELSVILLE-BALDWIN BEACH (Windward), KAHEKILI BEACH PARK (Ka'anapali)

BIG ISLAND

KIHILO BLACK SAND BEACH
This wild state beach is next to Blue Lagoon. Historical sites and ponds are tucked away in the margins of the backshore, along with a few cottages and mega-homes.

Worth a Look: OLD AIRPORT BEACH (Kona)

AND THE WINNER IS ... If you want au naturel beachwalks KAUA'I is the clear choice. Oahu, surprisingly, is second place.

10. WHALES & WILDLIFE

During winter and early spring, you can see migrating humpbacks offshore just about anywhere. But where are the best places? Dolphins, big sea turtles, and Hawaii's endangered monk seals also draw admirers. Seabirds and shorebirds are a coastal alternative for birdwatchers.

KAUA'I

KILAUEA POINT NATIONAL WILDLIFE REFUGE
Fantastic location on a lighthouse bluff that is the most northerly land in the main island chain. On the same day you can see whales, dolphins, monk seals, a variety of seabirds and shorebirds, and endangered nene, the Hawaiian state bird. Free binoculars, small admission.

MAKAWEHI BLUFF FROM SHIPWRECK BEACH
Nesting shorebirds, whales, and dolphins may grace the view along a trail starting at the Grand Hyatt in Poipu.

KEALIA LOOKOUT
This is the place to see whales along the paved path from Kapa'a to Kealia Beach.

LONGHOUSE BEACH-KAWAI POINT.
Turtles share the waters at Prince Kuhio's snorkeling spot, while monk seals bask on the small beach. Nearby, where the road ends at Kawai Point, is a spot often top-ranked for Kaua'i whale sightings.

WAIAKALUA BEACHES
Look for monk seals on the sand, whales offshore, and seabirds buzzing the airways.

Worth a Look: LARSENS BEACH (monk seals, seabirds), KAHILI BEACH (whales, seabirds), AHUKINI LANDING (turtles), SALT POND BEACH PARK (dolphins, Pa'akahi Point)

Nene, Kilauea Refuge, Kauai

OAHU

KAHALA MANDARIN ORIENTAL
Interactive dolphin school at the resort's lagoon is a freebie for visitors who want to wander by.

MAKAPU'U LIGHTHOUSE ROAD
Whales are the featured critter from this up-high hike that separates the windward and leeward shores.

LAIE POINT STATE WAYSIDE
A low finger of land sticks into wild seas, pointing at a seabird island sanctuary.

KAENA POINT
Laysan albatross waddle about in native grasses. The wild current at the point gets swim-bys from whales.

Worth a Look: SEA LIFE PARK (dolphins), LANIAKEA BEACH (turtles), MAKUA BEACH (dolphins), WAIKIKI AQUARIUM (monk seals)

MAUI

McGREGOR POINT
Bring a folding chair and join the crowd for sunset whale viewing at a number of elevated roadside turnouts.

KAHAKULOA HEAD
Kind of hard to find this windward nook at an island landmark, but whales cruise by close enough to hear them exhale.

HAWAIIAN ISLANDS HUMPBACK WHALE SANCTUARY
Interpretive displays and knowledgeable staff enrich the viewing.

OLOWALU LANDING
Whales breach and roll on the way toward Lahaina. Turtles hang closer to shore.

OHAI TRAIL
Watch for whales from the green bluffs of north Maui, with Molokai across the channel.

WETLANDS BOARDWALK-KEALIA POND REFUGE
The new boardwalk convenient for bird viewing along Ma'alaea Bay.

Worth a Look: KANAHA POND WILDLIFE SANCTUARY (Kahului, shorebirds), HULU AND MOKE'EHIA ISLANDS (windward, seabirds), CHANGS POINT (Makena Landing, turtles)

BIG ISLAND

PUAKO-PANIAU BAY
Be careful not to step on the turtles at the multiple access points of this shoreline.

BLUE LAGOON
A saltwater crust turns the turtles' shells white along the banks of the turquoise lagoon. A dip in the water restores their green-gold buff.

Humpback whale, Maui

LAPAKAHI HISTORICAL PARK TRAIL
The trail is just high enough for a seaward view of whales.

HILTON RESORT
Lounge on the grassy bank of the resort's lagoon and watch the staff of Dolphin Quest do their thing. No admission charged.

HONOMALINO BEACH
Spinner dolphin go fishing at this wild beach.

PUNALU'U BLACK SAND BEACH
Turtles haul out to the delight of busloads of tourists.

KAPALAOA BEACH
A short walk from Anaeho'omalu Bay will likely pass turtles.

Worth a Look: KEALAKEKUA BAY (dolphins), PU'UHONUA O HONAUNAU (Kealakekua Bay, whales, turtles)

AND THE WINNERS ARE ... For whale watching, go with MAUI, with the Big Island a second choice. For seabirds and monk seals, KAUA'I is the clear choice. Turtle lovers will definitely want to go for the BIG ISLAND, with Maui second. BIG ISLAND is also the choice to see dolphins.

11. WAVES FOR THE BIG BOYS
Pros come from around the globe to test their skills.

Photo: Robert Braun/BillabongXXL.com

Surfer Dan Moore takes on Jaws, Maui

KAUA'I

KINGS & QUEENS

The big Queens break far off Hanalei Pier is 'only' 25 to 30 feet. Kings is an outer reef, breaking at swells of 50 feet and higher—ridden for the first time only recently by Titus Kinimaka.

Worth a Look: LONGHOUSE (Prince Kuhio, summer)

OAHU

PIPELINE

The most famous wave in the world—a giant reef-breaking tube not far off the sands of North Shore's Ehukai Beach Park. Part of the professional circuit.

WAIMEA

Home to the Quiksilver In Memory of Eddie Aikau Big Wave Invitational and other professional surfing competitions.

HALEIWA

Doesn't get the press of its North Shore pro-circuit cousins, but the best surfers flock to the 'surfing capital of the world.'

SUNSET BEACH

Tour buses pack the pullout at this big sandy North Shore beach to take a look at the heavy surf and its intrepid riders.

MAKAHA BEACH

This West Side local boys' beach is home to several surfing competitions, including the incomparable Buffalo's Big Board Classic. Home surf for the Keaulana family and the late Rell Sunn, queen of the longboard.

Worth a Look: VELZYLAND (North Shore)

MAUI

JAWS

World tow-surfing king Laird Hamilton honed his skills at this massive break off the bluffs south of Paia.

HONOLUA BAY

An awesome right-break brings some of the best to this north end bay.

BIG ISLAND

Not known for big-wave pro surfing.

AND THE WINNER IS ... OAHU is the surfing capital of the world, as well as Hawaii.

12. RELIABLE SPOTS FOR GOOD SURFERS

There are usually waves, big or small, depending on the day.
In general, north shores break bigger in winter; south shores in summer.

KAUA'I

PINETREES

Shallow sand creates a near-shore wave machine in the center of Hanalei Bay. A grove of ironwoods marks the spot.

KALIHIWAI BAY

Local boys and girls love the bay-mouth right break at this beach park near Kilauea. Watch out for the head-on with the cliff.

WAIOHAI BEACH

Wedges form in the middle of the sands of Poipu, at a reef not too far offshore. Best in summer.

Worth a Look: BRENNECKES (Poipu), DAVIDSONS (Kekaha), WAIKOKO (Hanalei Bay), CANNONS (Haena Beach Park), INFINITIES (Pakala Beach, near Waimea), HIDEAWAYS (Princeville), KALAPAKI BAY (Nawiliwili)

OAHU

KAUNALA BEACH

Nearby Sunset gets the street traffic, but locals and internationals alike head for this bay's best break, Velzyland.

TRACKS

Tiers of medium breaks draw surfers from suburban Honolulu to this West Side pullout, at the power plant near Ko Olina.

CLIFFS

Surfers carry boards down many steps to a beach park set below Diamond Head.

CANOES

Reliable rideability near the big rack of boards at the Waikiki Beach Center—in the heart of it all.

CHUNS REEF

You'll see the cars collect at the highway shoulder at this chancy reef break midway between Haleiwa and Waimea Bay.

Makaha Beach, Oahu

Oahu Surfing Spots, cont'd—

COCKROACH BAY
A shallow reef draws short-boarders to this bay near Makap'u Beach Park.

MAILE BEACH PARK
Competitions are held at this easy-access West Side beach.

HAWAII KAI
Kaisers, China Wall, and Pillars are few breaks off the tricky coastline at Portlock.

SWABBIELAND
Nimitz Beach Park in Ewa is an underrated surfing venue.

Worth a Look: SILVA CHANNEL (Mokuleia Coast), PRAY FOR SURF (Makua, West Side), PINBALLS, (Waimea), BROWNS-CROMWELLS (Black Point), ALA MOANA BEACH PARK (Honolulu), SUICIDES (Diamond Head Beach Park), POINT PANIC (Kaka'ako Waterfront, Honolulu)

MAUI

LAHAINA SEAWALL
A man-made jetty has helped the natural harbor break.

HO'OKIPA
Though it can get blown out, the right break at the rough point stays true to form often enough to be the pick on the windward coast.

MA'ALAEA BAY
Check it in the summer, at two breaks: Mud Flats and Breakwater

BIG BEACH
When summer's Kona surf arrives, surfers head to the south end of Makena State Park.

IRONWOODS
Winter is the best ride for the rolling tiers into Oneloa Beach, between the Ritz Carlton and Kapalua Bay.

Worth a Look: LAUNIUPOKO BEACH PARK (south of Lahaina), MALA WHARF (Lahaina), PAUKUKA-LAO (Kahului), PO'OLENALENA (Wailea)

BIG ISLAND

LYMANS
A sweet left slide into Kona's Holualoa Bay has seen board riders for centuries, as evidenced by an overgrown surfing heiau on the point.

HONOLI'I BEACH PARK
All the boys and girls board-carry down the path to Hilo's (east Hawaii's) best surfing beach.

PINETREES
Just south of the Kona Airport was the site of a landmark mangrove (not pine trees) but even that tree has been chopped. Reliable waves remain.

Worth a Look: KAHALU'U BAY (Kona), BOWLS-ISAAC HALE (Puna), WAIPIO BEACH, HO'OKENA BEACH PARK (south Kona), PAPIHA POINT (Kua Bay), KALOKO POND (Kona), BANYANS (Kailua), 3-MILES (Hilo)

AND THE WINNER IS ... No surprise, OAHU, is where you'll find legions of surfers. Kaua'i and Maui have plenty of breaks, and so does the Big Island, though it's a long drive among them.

13. LEARN-TO-SURF BEACHES
Instructors can get you up and riding the near-shore surf.

KAUA'I

BLACK POT BEACH
Gentle waves, shallow water, and local-guy instructors add up to top marks for this Hanalei Bay beach by the pier.

POIPU BEACH
Several schools operate on the sunny resort beach.

OAHU

WAIKIKI BEACH CENTER
Right in the center of things on Waikiki. You'll find surf-shack schools and also sole proprietors

PUAENA
Haleiwa, the low-key center of commerce for the North Shore, has one of the islands' best beginner beaches, with a good surf school close by

WAIMANALO BEACH PARK
A long run on sand-breaking, near-shore waves.

MALAEKAHANA RECREATION AREA
The Kahuku Section, at the north of the recreation area, is a good place for visiting surfers to test Oahu's waters.

WHITE PLAINS BEACH PARK
Mellow beach scene in Ewa draws beginning and intermediate surfers.

MAUI

COVE PARK
Sweet little cove in Kihei with junior waves inshore and surf outfitters nearby.

LAUNUIPOKO BEACH PARK
A little reefy, but a lot of people stand on the board for the first time at this beach park south of Lahaina.

PUAMANA BEACH PARK
Another low-key locals beach park south of Lahaina with forgiving waves.

BIG ISLAND
Not the best island to learn.

AND THE WINNER IS ... A clean sweep for OAHU in the surfing category. But Maui and Kaua'i have offerings for learners.

14. BODYBOARDING
Belly on the board, rolling in the white water.

KAUA'I

KEALIA BEACH PARK
A long run of sand near Kapa'a has a multi-tiered, near-shore break that gives bodyboarders a frothy ride. Always a scene.

KALIHIWAI BEACH PARK
A sandy shore break at the stream mouth creates a bodyboarding park.

SHIPWRECK BEACH
Submerged rocks and shallow reef don't bother the boys at this Poipu beach, near the Grand Hyatt.

OAHU

SANDY BEACH
The renowned action beach for highschoolers and up is the site for top-end bodyboard competitions.

POUNDERS
Beginners won't want to try the at-the-bluff break at Laie Beach Park—but the hot surfers can't wait.

Poipu Beach, Kauai

Yokohama Bay, Oahu

THE WALL

The concrete breakwater in Waikiki is bodyboard central. Surfers peel off the wave before doing a head on.

YOKOHAMA BAY

West Side guys gather to test the wild bay's sandy shore break.

MAKAPUʻU BEACH PARK

South Windward surf was home to Oahu's first-ever bodyboard competitions that began in the 1950s.

BELLOWS FIELD BEACH PARK

This Waimanalo park gets popular on weekends—the only days it is open.

PAPAONEONE BEACH

Check out the barrels at this tourist beach behind the Hawaiian Princess in Makaha.

HUKILAU BEACH PARK

Friendly scene at a scenic, private park in Laie.

MAUI

LITTLE BEACH

Though nude sunbathing (unlawful) is the claim to fame at Makena's smaller beach, bodyboarding waves are reason enough to visit.

BALDWIN BEACH PARK

The perfect Hawaii wave scene. Baldwin is a gathering place.

KOKI BEACH

In Hana, this red-sand beach is not normally crowded.

D.T. FLEMMING BEACH PARK

Rough break is no deterrent for bodyboarders at the north Kapalua beach.

Flipping at Makapuu, Oahu

BIG ISLAND

SPINNERS

In the heart of Kona, this rocky right break into little Oneo Bay is where bodyboarding got its start.

WHITE SANDS BEACH PARK

Winter surf usually wipes out the sand at the Kona beach, but competitions (bodysurfing) are held here when the conditions are right.

KEALAKEKUA HISTORICAL PARK

Shore break attracts local boys for their daily fix.

Worth a Look: KAUNAOA BEACH (Mauna Kea Resort)

AND THE WINNER IS ... OAHU dominates surfing. But bodyboarders will have a ticket to ride on all the islands.

15. BEST PLACES TO WATCH SURFERS
It's a free-flowing spectator sport that can be addictive. Watch from all angles.

KAUA'I
KALIHIWAI OVERLOOK
A turnout at the guardrail on the way down to the beach park gives you an overhead look at surfers riding some of the islands' best waves.

HANALEI PIER
Surfers come peeling by on the tamer inshore break. Keen eyes will focus on Queens break, farther out on the reef.

BEACH HOUSE (LONGHOUSE)
Summer is the time to gather on the grassy bluffs by the restaurant in Prince Kuhio.

Worth a Look: FORT ALEXANDER-HIDEAWAYS (Princeville)

OAHU
PIPELINE
Sloping sand, with beach trees for shade, is the perfect amphitheater. The famous barrel break is close to shore.

KAPAHULU GROIN
Take a walk out on the concrete breakwater near Kapiolani Park to be close to the action in Waikiki.

KEPUHI PONT, MAKAHA
An obscure neighborhood beach access gets you close to the rollicking reef break on the West Side.

HALEIWA BREAKWATER
Between the beach park and the harbor.

WAIMEA BAY
The parking lot is big, but it gets full. Park at the church on the hill and walk down to the guardrail opening for the good seats.

KAKA'AKO WATERFRONT PARK
The paved promenade is the spot to watch 'em ride Point Panic, on the Honolulu side of Ala Moana Beach Park.

KOKO KAI BEACH PARK
A series of quick turns in Portlock (Hawaii Kai) gets you to a bluff that is the beach access—watch out for rogue waves.

MAKAPU'U BEACH PARK
A rock jutting into the water in the middle of the bay provides a ringside seat.

POUNDERS BLUFF
Step onto the bluff at Laie Beach Park and you're close enough to watch the surfers' eyes get big when they get ready to hit the wall.

Worth a Look: WATERHOUSE ESTATE (Papaoneone Beach, Makaha), SUNSET BEACH (North Shore)

MAUI
HONOLUA BAY
Take the dirt turnout where all the cars park at the north end of the bay, and walk down the cliff face a short distance to the eagle's perch.

HO'OKIPA LOOKOUT
Wave gawkers gather at the signed lookout on the south end of the beach; on the north end is viewing for windsurfers.

LAHAINA SEAWALL
Take a walk out to get close to two nice breaks and also to check out the colorful boats in the harbor.

JAWS
Windward Peahi Point is a primo grandstand to watch the lords of big-wave tow surfing, but the huge surf only arrives a couple times yearly.

BIG ISLAND
HOLUALOA BAY
With a little effort (walk a bulkhead, skirt an overgrown shore) you get to the big view at Lymans, a left break at the mouth of the bay.

HALE HALAWAI
You can sit in a restaurant in Kona or take a seat along the walkway to get up close to the translucent barrels at Spinners.

HONOLI'I BEACH PARK
The walkway down from the street gives up the good view of Hilo's best surf spot.

KUEMANU HEIAU
The little church is the place to be for the reef break at Kahalu'u Bay, in Kona.

AND THE WINNER IS ... OAHU'S North Shore is surf city for spectators.

Pipeline, Oahu

16. WINDSURFING & KITE-BOARDING
Harnessing the wind, lots of colorful sails flitting around, behind, and over the waves.

KAUA'I

ANINI BEACH
The reef gives kite-boarders and windsurfers a protected, flat surface, but the wind is not totally reliable.

SHIPWRECK BEACH
Big swells and deep water await the fearless windsurfer.

FUJI BEACH
Kapa'a's new entry into the kite-boarding arena. Reef protects the shore.

OAHU

FLAT ISLAND-KAILUA BEACH PARK
Windsurfers join kayakers.

MOKULEIA BEACH PARK
A narrow strip of sand is the launch pad for game kite-boarders on the rough north coast.

MAUI

HO'OKIPA
This beach close to Paia on windward Maui is the birthplace of windsurfing. Wave jumping is required.

KANAHA BEACH PARK
Kite-boarders and windsurfers commandeer different ends of this beach near the airport. Quite a sight.

MAI POINA 'OE IAU BEACH PARK
Long name, big windsurfing, in North Kihei.

HAYCRAFT BEACH PARK
Wind whips over the isthmus at Ma'alaea Bay, fuel for windsurfers.

WAIEHU BEACH PARK
This hidden park just north of Wailuku is the next big thing for kite-boarders.

BIG ISLAND

ANAEHO'OMALU BAY
Windsurfers take off from the park, in Waikaloa.

KAPALAOA BEACH
Kite-boarders have taken to this beach a short walk from A-Bay in Waikaloa.

AND THE WINNER IS ... MAUI rules the islands for wind-in-your-sails sports.

Hookipa, Maui

17. KAYAKING: RIVER LAGOONS and OCEAN

KAUA'I
River lagoons

WAILUA RIVER – Outfitters and independents take the popular paddles to Secret Falls, Kamokulia Village.

HANALEI RIVER – Another outfitters route into the wildlife refuge beneath the north shore's green ridgelines.

HULEIA STREAM – A wide waterway from Nawiliwili Harbor flows past the ancient Menehune Fishpond and into the wildlife refuge. Scenes from *Jurassic Park* and *Raiders of the Lost Ark* were filmed here.

Wailua River, Kauai

WAIMEA AND HANAPEPE RIVERS– These west side rivers partway up red canyons see few paddlers—and no tours.

OTHER INLAND WATERWAYS– Inland slack waters at several beaches also invite an exotic paddle. Included are Lumahai River, Kalihiwai River, and Kilauea Stream are on the north side. Anahola and Kealia stream, on the east side near Kapa'a.

Ocean

NORTH SHORE – Paddlers head out Hanalei River to nearby by Pu'u Poa beach. The miles-long calm waters inside the reef at Anini Beach are also good. Napali Coast is spectacular—guide required.

POIPU – Paddle the coast toward the beach at Allerton Garden, a fairly mellow offshore route. Another adventure is from Mahaulepu Beach, near Poipu, to exclusive Kipu Kai Beach.

OAHU
River Lagoons: None
Ocean

WINDWARD – Several seabird islands close to shore make Windward prime kayak country. Rabbit Island is off Waimanalo, while photogenic Mokulua islands and Flat Island beckon from Kailua Beach Park. Farther up the coast are Chinaman's Hat (Mokoli'i Island) and Goat Island.

WAIKIKI – The several-mile resort beachfront is safe for kayakers, but you see more outrigger canoe and sailboats leaving Ala Wai Harbor.

MAUI
River lagoons: Nope
Ocean

LA PEROUSE BAY – A put-in for the shores of the Ahihi Kinau Natural Area Preserve, harsh lava-land not otherwise easily reached.

MAKENA LANDING – Cruise Turtle Town, Big Beach, and waters off the southern Wailea resorts coastline. You can also access these waters farther north, from Kihei Landing.

OLOWALU LANDING – This out-of-the-way put-in is a scenic option to visit the relatively tame waters on the northwest side of Maui. Ma'alaea Bay and several spots around Lahaina also work. Great inland views, and a few little bays and beaches.

HANA-KEANAE – See the Hana Highway and the majestic south tip near Hana. Easy put-ins, but you need to be experienced or go with a guide to safely enjoy this adventure.

BIG ISLAND
River lagoons: Not happening.
Ocean

ANAEHO'OMALU – A-Bay is the take off to reach the rugged coast that is pocketed with beach oases (one the campsite for author Paul Theroux). Best to have experience and good advice, or go with a guide.

HILO BAY – Enjoy the vast bay and Moku Ola (Coconut Island) from inside the long breakwater that protects the twice-hit bay from further tsunamis.

AND THE WINNERS ARE ... For river lagoons, **KAUA'I** is the winner, and not just by default. You can build an adventure vacation around paddling freshwater in Kaua'i.

Hey, all the islands have water around them, but **MAUI** offers the most opportunities for ocean-bound kayakers. Oahu has some beautiful and intriguing paddles as well. Kaua'i's Napali coast is the adventure paddle that tops them all.

Secret Falls, Wailua River, Kauai

18. MUSEUMS & GALLERIES
Some of the best in the world, and many sure to entertain, aloha-style.

KAUA'I

WAIOLI MISSION HOUSE
Be transported to 1841 by strolling across a green lawn in Hanalei to the modest mission house. Its gardens give way to taro fields and the sublime ramparts of Waioli Valley.

KAUA'I MUSEUM
Make sure to see the Kaua'i history exhibits in the annex attached to the historic museum building in Lihue.

GROVE FARM HOMESTEAD MUSEUM
The Wilcox missionary home, cottage, and gardens are tucked away in a Lihue neighborhood. A sense of place is preserved.

Worth a Look: KOKE'E MUSEUM (in the state park, Waimea Canyon)

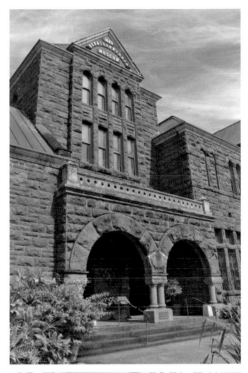

OAHU

BISHOP MUSEUM & SCIENCE LEARNING CENTER
Campuslike grounds, established in 1889, are a legacy of Princess Bernice Pauahi Bishop, the great-granddaughter of Kamehameha the Great. A science center opened in 2005 and the grand halls of the museum were renovated in 2006-07.

HONOLULU ACADEMY OF THE ARTS
Housed in an award-winning building of Mediterranean design are 40,000 works from Hawaii and around the world.

HAWAII MARITIME CENTER
In King David Kalakaua's former boathouse on Honolulu Harbor are an array of fanciful exhibits. Outside is the mooring for the Hokulea, the sailing canoe that today recreates historic Polynesian voyages.

US ARMY MUSEUM
A massive, subterranean artillery battery right on Waikiki.

NORTH SHORE SURF & CULTURAL MUSEUM
Haleiwa's homage to Surf City gets points for being quirky.

MISSION HOUSES MUSEUM
Near other attractions in Honolulu, these coral homes from 1830 (the city's first structures) are often overlooked.

QUEEN EMMA SUMMER PALACE
Modest home in Nu'uanu Valley Park that was the getaway for the queen and King Kamehameha IV. Original furnishings are intact.

Bishop Museum, Hawaii Maritime Center, Oahu

Worth a Look: TROPIC LIGHTNING MUSEUM
(Schofield Barracks), HAWAII STATE ART
MUSEUM (Honolulu), USS BOWFIN SUBMARINE
PARK (Pearl Harbor)

MAUI

BAILEY HOUSE MUSEUM
In the former Wailuku Female Seminary,
circa 1832, the museum is the highlight of a
historic-district stroll.

HALE PA'AHEO PRISON
Kids will love it inside the walls of the "stuck-
in-irons house," a vestige of the bawdy
whaling days of Lahaina in the mid-1800s.

BALDWIN MUSEUM & COURTHOUSE
Take a history break at this missionary house
in the middle of the tourist hubbub of
downtown Lahaina

Worth a Look: WO HING MUSEUM (Lahaina)

BIG ISLAND

EVA PARKER WOODS MUSEUM
A tiny cottage next to the beach and ponds of
ancient Kalahiupua'a Village, on the grounds
of the Mauna Lani Resort. Try to attend one
of Danny Akaka's (free) full-moon Talk Story
performances.

VOLCANO ART CENTER
Local fine art in the original historic building
at Hawaii Volcanoes National Park. Pele's
Hula platform is outside.

HULIHE'E PALACE
Beachside former governor's home is the
centerpiece of Kona, and across the street
from Mokuaikaue Church, Hawaii's first
dating from 1820.

JAGGAR MUSEUM
Next to volcano observatory in the national
park, full of volcanology displays, and in an
otherworldly setting on the rim of Kilauea
Caldera.

KONA COFFEE LIVING HISTORY FARM
Nationally recognized re-creation of a
seven-acre Japanese coffee and macadamia
farm of the early 1920s.

Worth a Look: ISAACS ART CENTER (Waimea),
KAUPULEHU CULTURAL CENTER (Four Seasons
Resort), KONA HISTORICAL SOCIETY-GREEN-
WELL STORE, PACIFIC TSUNAMI MUSEUM (Hilo),
ONIZUKA SPACE CENTER (Kona), LYMAN HOUSE
MUSEUM (Hilo)

**AND THE WINNER IS ... OAHU runs away with
this category, but the Big Island has a breadth of
offerings.**

Hulihee Palace, Big Island; USS Bowfin Submarine Park, Oahu

Iolani Palace, Oahu

19. ATTRACTIONS & VISITOR CENTERS
Aquariums, national parks, sugar cane plantations, Hawaiian cowboys, volcanoes, tsunamis, astronomy, coffee, marine mammals ...

KAUA'I

KILAUEA POINT NATIONAL WILDLIFE SANCTUARY
This lighthouse bluff is the northernmost land of the major islands. On the same day you may see whales, dolphins, and monk seals, along with many species of soaring and nesting shorebirds.

SMITH'S FERN GROTTO BOAT TOURS
A kitschy classic, run by the same family since the 1940s. A hula show on a riverboat up the Wailua ends at the famed ferny cavern, where visitors are serenaded in a natural amphitheater.

KILOHANA PLANTATION
A historic-replica railway ride started rolling in 2007, the topper on this estate with restaurant, shops, and historical displays.

GAY & ROBINSON SUGAR PLANTATION
A ride through the red dirt fields and into the processing plant of one of Hawaii's two remaining operations.

Worth a Look: KAUA'I COFFEE COMPANY VISITORS CENTER (Port Allen), GUAVA KAI PLANTATION (Kilauea)

OAHU

USS ARIZONA MEMORIAL AT PEARL HARBOR
Among the top attractions in the world. A vibrant visitors center and a moving movie are the setup for a boat ride to the memorial that resides over the battleships sunk on the 'Day of Infamy.' Oil still seeps from the Arizona.

POLYNESIAN CULTURAL CENTER
Yes, it's pricey and Hawaii's number-one paid attraction. But PCC is the real deal, where Polynesian traditions of many island nations are on display around a 43-acre lagoon on the Windward Coast in Laie.

IOLANI PALACE
The flame of the monarchy has never been extinguished at the downtown home of the royals—which had electricity before the White House.

HAWAII'S PLANTATION VILLAGE
Small village re-creation delivers a big impact, with the details of the many cultures that comprised Hawaii's sugar workforce.

Polynesian Cultural Center, Oahu; Maui Ocean Center's walk-through tube; Humpback Whale National Marine Sancturary, Maui; Waikiki Aquarium

Attractions & Visitor Centers, cont'd—

WAIKIKI AQUARIUM

Coral is exported around the world from this University of Hawaii-run seaside facility. Displays are intricately arranged. You can also get personal with resident monk seals.

DORIS DUKE'S SHANGRI LA

A beautiful and fabulously wealthy heiress built this ornate mansion and hang-out for the rich and arty of the early 1900s. Located on Black Point, extending below Diamond Head.

OAHU MARKET-MAUNAKEA MARKETPLACE

Mind-boggling array of seafood, produce, tropical fruits, and exotic foodstuffs in the heart of Honolulu's Chinatown.

Worth a Look: HAWAIIAN RAILWAY SOCIETY (Kapolei), ALI'IOLANI HALE (Honolulu), KUALOA RANCH (Windward), SEA LIFE PARK (Waimanalo), USS MISSOURI (Pearl Harbor), TROPICAL FARMS-ALI'I TOUR (Windward), ALOHA STADIUM SWAP MEET, HONOLULU ZOO (Kapiolani Park), DUKE'S CANOE CLUB (Waikiki), ALOHA TOWER (Honolulu), HURL (HAWAII UNDERWATER RESEARCH LABORATORY, Waimanalo)

MAUI

MAUI OCEAN CENTER

Scuba dive without getting wet in an expansive sea tunnel, then pop up to visit sea turtles and tiger sharks. This is America's largest tropical aquarium, and a tribute to marine life of the Pacific.

HALEAKALA VISITORS CENTER-RED HILL PAVILION

The view is everything at these two outposts atop the 10,000-foot volcano.

ULUPALAKUA RANCH

Wander the arboretum and sample the products of Tedeschi Winery at this upcountry estate that was a favorite of King David Kalakaua and author Robert Louis Stevenson.

HUMPBACK WHALE NATIONAL MARINE SANCTUARY

The north Kihei shore is the place to keep an eye out for the big mammals and learn about them.

Worth a Look: MAUI SWAP MEET (Kahului)

BIG ISLAND

MAUNA KEA OBSERVATORIES

The western world gazes to the heavens from a dozen observatories at the top of the world. Ancient Hawaiians did the same, and the short walk to the summit is marked only by a modest shrine.

KILAUEA VISITORS CENTER-VOLCANO HOUSE

The Hawaii Volcanoes National Park center, renovated in 2005, is alive with interpretive displays and rangers giving precious info about current lava flows. Across the way, the venerable Volcano House hotel and restaurant gives up an awesome view of the caldera

MOKUPAPAPA CENTER FOR HAWAII'S REMOTE CORAL REEFS

Hands-on displays about a little-known place. The center is tucked into the storefronts in historic Hilo. Give 'em an A for presentation and originality.

ROYAL KONA COFFEE-KONA COFFEE UCC CO-OP

Bottomless sample urns of Kona's fabled brew lubricate a sky-high view of Kealakekua Bay. Bay View Farms and Blue Sky are two other top coffee stops.

Worth a Look: MAUNA LOA MACADAMIA NUT VISITORS CENTER (Hilo), IMILOA ASTRONOMY CENTER (Hilo), ONIZUKA CENTER FOR ASTRONOMY (Kona Airport), PANAEWA RAIN FOREST ZOO (Hilo)

AND THE WINNER IS ... With a wealth of selections, OAHU is a clear winner. Big Island nudges Kaua'i for runner-up.

20. HAWAIIAN TEMPLES & ANCIENT SITES

Polynesian mariners came from the South Pacific, beginning in about 100 AD—constructing petroglyphs, shrines, and temples. All of the listings are religious sites: treat them as you would a church.

KAUA'I

KAULUOLAKA HEIAU (HULA TEMPLE)
Lofted above crashing seas at gateway to the Napali coast is the most sacred and important hula platform in all of Hawaii.

POLIAHU HEIAU-THE BELLSTONE
The third of the seven sacred heiaus that were built by earliest Kauaians, stretching from the river mouth at the coast to Mount Waialeale, this one is on a high bluff above the river.

Worth a Look: MENEHUNE DITCH (Waimea), MENEHUNE FISHPOND (Nawiliwili), MALAE HEIAU (Wailua), WAIOPILI HEIAU (Poipu)

Puuhonua O Honaunau National Park, Big Island

Puuhonua O Honaunau National Park, Big Island; Kaneaki Heiau, Oahu

OAHU

KANEAKI HEIAU
Although you need to sign in during special hours at a gated community to see it, this heiau stands in the wilds of Makaha Valley. Stopover spot for Kamehameha's ill-fated invasion of Kaua'i.

PU'U O MAHUKA HEIAU STATE MONUMENT
A large structure above the North Shore's Waimea Bay, from which signal fires could be seen on Kaua'i.

ULUPO HEIAU STATE MONUMENT
Ironically situated next to neighborhood homes in Kailua, this large heiau foundation remains intact, and marshlands (former fishponds) below are still open space.

HALE O LONO HEIAU
Recently unearthed, this heiau is at the gateway of Waimea Valley Audubon Center, which is also the site of many ruins and a magnificent garden-arboretum.

Worth a Look: KUKAILOKO BIRTHSTONES STATE MONUMENT (Wahiawa), KEAIWA HEIAU STATE RECREATION AREA (Pearl City)

MAUI

PI'ILANIHALE HEIAU
Built in the 1500s, this king's temple rises with the drama of an Aztec ruin. A bonus is its setting, within a national tropical botanical garden.

KING'S TRAIL FROM KEONEOIO VILLAGE
It's not hard to imagine early Hawaiians marching this road through the jagged lava fields of south Maui, beginning at La Perouse Bay.

HALEKI'I-PIHANA HEIAUS STATE MONUMENT
Giant heiaus rise above warehouses and homes in Wailuku.

Worth a Look: OLOWALU PETROGLYPHS, HALEHAKU HEIAU (near Huelo)

BIG ISLAND

PU'UHONUA O HONAUNAU NATIONAL PARK
Artisans are normally on hand to give even more authenticity to the preserved place of refuge and dwelling place of royalty. Ki'ilae Village coastal trail is nearby.

Hawaiian Temples & Ancient Sites, cont'd—

KING KAMEHAMEHA BIRTHSITE-MO'OKINI HEIAU
A wide-open, windswept setting gives these sites a timeless feel. Maui rises across the channel.

WAIKALOA PETROGLYPH PRESERVE
Next to a golf course and luxury condominiums, a vast field of rock etchings tells the story of the many generations of warriors and travelers who encamped at the border of two Big Island districts.

KALOKO-HONOKOHAU NATIONAL HISTORIC PARK
New discoveries are still taking place: petroglyphs, mysterious rock mounds, burial sites, heiaus, fishponds, and shrines. In the early 1800s, a lava flow buried much of what were Kamehameha's gardens, just north of Kona.

PU'UKOHOLA HEIAU NATIONAL MONUMENT
The huge war temple where Kamehameha's cousin, a rival, was killed, giving Kamehameha rule over the Big Island.

LAPAKAHI STATE HISTORICAL PARK
Large coastal village was one of Hawaii's first preserved villages, located on the west coast of Kohala.

KANE'ELE'ELE HEIAU-NINOLE SHRINES
Near Black Sand Beach on the east shore are a number of shrines, unsigned and seldom visited by tourists.

HIKIAU HEIAU, KEALAKEKUA HISTORICAL PARK
Where Captain James Cook was hailed as the god Lono and, after he was slain, where his bones were honored.

PUAKO PETROGLYPHS
A large, marked field is surrounded by a number of other etchings in the wilds of a kiawe forest.

KAUPULEHU PETROGLYPHS
A boardwalk makes the viewing easy, but you have to make arrangements with Kona Village resort in order to visit.

PU'U LOA PETROGLYPHS
This very ancient site was spared from the recent flows near the coast of Hawaii Volcanoes National Park.

Worth a Look: KING'S TRAIL (Kua Bay), KALALEA HEIAU-SOUTH POINT CANOE LADDERS

AND THE WINNER IS ... Kamehameha's **BIG ISLAND** is a hands-down choice. Fresh discoveries await the adventuresome traveler.

Puukohola Heiau National Monument, Big Island

21. BOTANICAL GARDENS
Many acres of flowers, shrubs, and, trees—somebody's brainchild.

KAUA'I

ALLERTON NATIONAL TROPICAL BOTANICAL GARDEN

The life's work of the late Robert Allerton, the grandfather of Hawaii's gardens, has been an inspiration for movie directors. The roots of America's tropical gardens are here.

NA AINA KAI BOTANICAL GARDENS AND SCULPTURE PARK

"Just" 20 years in the making, the sprawling ocean-bluff garden uses some 100 well-placed bronze statuary as focal points of botanical dioramas.

LIMAHULI NATIONAL TROPICAL BOTANICAL GARDEN

As close to Eden as you can get on earth. Garden terraces and a winding path lead into the tiny valley beneath fanciful peaks.

McBRIDE NATIONAL TROPICAL BOTANICAL GARDEN

Take a stroll through Allerton's neighboring garden, a streamside exhibition of native, exotic, and endangered plants.

SMITHS TROPICAL PARADISE

An underrated offering beside the Smith's luau site and boat rides on the Wailua River. Footbridges span lagoons amid flowering tropicals and cultural displays.

Worth a Look: MOIR GARDENS (Poipu, free)

OAHU

LYON ARBORETUM

Pleasingly set on a treetop knoll below the steep wall of the Ko'olau Mountains. Stroll garden paths and arboretum trails. Free admission.

WAIMEA VALLEY AUDUBON CENTER

Historically an ancient village—many remnants remain—the refuge now holds some three-dozen individual gardens along a large stream. You can walk a couple miles or more to see it all, including the waterfall and swimmable pool at the upper end.

HO'OMALUHIA BOTANICAL GARDEN

The high wall of the Ko'olau Range is the backdrop for 400 acres, with a large pond, hiking trails, and a number of individual gardens. Free admission.

KOKO CRATER BOTANICAL GARDENS

Weird cacti, birds, an array of palms, and a forest of plumeria are rimmed by 1,000-foot crater walls. Admission is free.

FOSTER BOTANICAL GARDEN.

Mammoth trees are the calling card for this historic garden, set near a freeway in downtown Honolulu.

WAHIAWA BOTANICAL GARDEN

A new visitors center is the highlight of a 2005 rehab of these 27 acres of mature trees and flowering plants terraced over a deep ravine. Free admission.

Worth a Look: SENATOR FONG'S PLANTATION GARDEN (Windward), LILIUOKALANI BOTANICAL GARDENS (Honolulu)

Allerton Garden, Kauai

Botanical Gardens, cont'd—

MAUI

KEANAE ARBORETUM
A green respite on the Hana Highway features tropical trees from both sides of the equator. A Hawaiian garden heads the arboretum, and hikers can keep on going up the valley. Free.

KAHANU NATIONAL TROPICAL BOTANICAL GARDENS
A large heiau on site can overshadow the gardens, which include a display of the 27 "canoe plants" brought by the original Polynesians. Surrounded by a forest of pandanus and breadfruit trees.

KEPANIWAI HERITAGE GARDENS
A county park along a stream at the foot of Iao Valley features coco palms, taro, banyans, and Polynesian flora planted around huts and buildings that represent various cultural traditions. Free admission. The Hawaii Nature Center is next door.

GARDEN OF EDEN
Get coastal views, including one that was the opening sequence of *Jurassic Park*—midway along the Hana Highway.

IAO VALLEY BOTANICAL GARDEN
Streamside terraces reside below the famous needle at the state park. Free admission.

Worth a Look: ALI'I KULA LAVENDER GARDEN, KULA BOTANICAL GARDEN

Keanae Arboretum, Maui

BIG ISLAND

HAWAII TROPICAL BOTANICAL GARDEN
A boardwalk winds down past a waterfall. Paths wander through a beautifully complex array of flora. The gardens abut two scenic coves, joined by a coastal trail.

LILIUOKALANI GARDENS
A Japanese-designed park with footbridges at the edge of Hilo Bay, with a longer footbridge to Moku Ola (Coconut Island) steps away. Admission is free.

WORLD BOTANICAL GARDEN
The lookout of Umauma Falls and a streamside stroll nudge this effort into the top 20.

Worth a Look: PANAWEA RAINFOREST ZOO (Hilo), AMY B.H. GREENWELL ETHNOBOTANICAL GARDEN (Captain Cook)

AND THE WINNER IS ... KAUA'I, the Garden Island, has three of America's five national tropical gardens. Oahu takes second place.

Hawaii Tropical Botanical Garden, Big Island

22. WALK-AROUND TOURIST TOWNS

Shave ice, tee-shirts, cuisine, cocktails, cafes, art, trinkets, historic sites, surf shops, bikinis, locomoco, and people watching.

Waikiki, Oahu

KAUA'I

HANALEI
Low-key artsy shops, outfitters, and local-style restaurants are nestled between Hanalei Bay, Waioli Valley, and the Hanalei River. You can't beat it for sandy-footed chic.

KAPA'A
The hemp-set and locals create a nice mix of no-glitz tourism. Nice coastal path and grid of beach cottages. Fun nightlife.

HANAPEPE
Art, funk, and heritage balance out at this west side town along a river. Friday evenings are open-house art night.

KOLOA
An old sugar plantation town up the hill from Poipu Beach has more than meets the eye.

Worth a Look: WAIMEA, NAWILIWILI HARBOR

OAHU

WAIKIKI
Diamond Head lords over high-rise resorts and designer shops along two miles of beach-front. There is only one Waikiki.

HONOLULU
Heritage meets cosmopolitan in one of the world's best walking cities.

HALEIWA
Though lacking a centrality, Haleiwa has enough Old-Hawaii charm and surfer-cool to be worthy of being the North Shore's primary hangout.

ALA MOANA SHOPPING CENTER
A garishly fantastic multi-level fashion mall across the street from a huge beach park—between Waikiki and Honolulu.

CHINATOWN
Rough around the edges, real to the core, full of treats for the senses. (Part of Honolulu.)

MAUI

LAHAINA
Historically vibrant, alive with libation and shopping—and artfully set beneath Maui's mountains and alongside a working harbor.

PAIA
Traffic in town detracts from this hangout called the windsurfing capital of the world. Back-to-earth style mixes with the casual-society set at a range of restaurants and shops.

MAKAWAO
Maui's cowboy town draws artists and Hollywood types, along with some of the island's gentry. Pleasant surprise and getting better.

WAILUKU
Historic buildings help the old section in an effort to redevelop.

Hanapepe, Kauai

Walk-Around Tourist Towns, cont'd—

BIG ISLAND

HILO

Old Hilo Town is graced with dilapidated personality, seaside parks, and romantic-noir intrigue. Right on Hilo Bay and the river that separates Mauna Loa from Mauna Kea.

KAILUA-KONA

Quaint and historical, but also drenched with cotton-candy tourism and nick-knack shopping. Similar to Lahaina.

HAWI-KAPA'AU

The north shore community has the charm to seduce visitors. Part of a well-rounded day trip.

Worth a Look: HOLUALOA (above Kona), KEALAKEKUA-CAPTAIN COOK, HONOKA'A (AND HAMAKUA SUGAR CAMPS)

AND THE WINNER IS ... OAHU is on a scale apart from the neighbor islands. Kaua'i, Maui, and the Big Island tie for second depending on your taste, though Maui is the clear choice for fine dining and high-end shopping.

Kailua-Kona, Big Island; Leis for sale, Maui; Surfboard parking, Haleiwa, Oahu; Hilo's Palace Theater, Big Island

Lahaina, Maui

23. SWANK RESORTS

A blend of architecture, galleries, décor, fine dining, shops, and poolside gardenscapes. Hawaii has many of the world's best—both destination resorts and resort strips.

KAUA'I

PRINCEVILLE HOTEL
> A great wall of glass frames Hanalei Bay and the jagged ridges of Napali: The best resort view in Hawaii.

GRAND HYATT KAUA'I RESORT
> Elegant without being ostentatious, with Asian-inspired architecture that has created both grand spaces and quiet nooks.

MARRIOTT KALAPAKI BAY
> Lagoon, pool-view balconies, and nearby lighthouses, beaches, and yacht harbor give the Marriott all-around points. Rooms aren't as good as the environ.

OAHU

WAIKIKI
> No single resort wins the big prize, but Royal Hawaiian and Moana Surfrider are Waikiki's originals that retain old-style charm—though now they are swallowed by shopping and parking structures. The Halekulani, all about Hawaiiana and interior decoration, is also one of the granddames. Start at Hilton Hawaiian Village and walk toward Diamond Head.

GRAND KO OLINA RESORT
> Beaches and resort grounds—as well as a planned huge aquarium and shopping center—are testament of the tropical fantasy that money and machines can create.

MAUI

FOUR SEASONS AT MANELE BAY
AND LODGE LANAI AT KOELE
> Not really fair to give Maui the points, since these beauties are a ferry ride away on Lanai.

GRAND WAILEA-FOUR SEASONS
WAILEA-FAIRMONT KEA LANI
> Taken together, Wailea's best will entertain visitors who duck into the resorts along a beachfront path. Rated by travel magazines as among the world's best.

KA'ANAPALI
> The Sheraton and Hilton anchor a paved path. All the ingredients are there: great beaches, high-end shopping, restaurants, and a blend of gardens and architecture.

Worth a Look: RITZ CARLTON (Kapalua)

Grand Hyatt Kauai Resort

BIG ISLAND

HILTON WAIKALOA

Monorail, lagoon boat ride, dophin pools, and museumlike decorations make the Hilton a stand out among exorbitant Hawaiian resorts. Bring the family and spend the day.

MAUNA LANI-FAIRMONT ORCHID

Situated about .25-mile apart, these posh beauties feature a series of great beaches, coastal trails, lake-sized ponds and arboretum, and a history park. Guests don't need to leave.

FOUR SEASONS HUALALAI

Downplayed elegance. Coastal path leads to Kona Village (resort). Museum on-site is a surprise.

MAUNA KEA

Artfully set on Kaunaoa Bay, the Mauna Kea set the standard when built by Laurance Rockefeller in 1965. The earthquake of 2006 closed the resort, causing two year's worth of repair work.

Worth a Look: KING KAMEHAMEHA HOTEL (Kailua-Kona), KEAHOU SHERATON, KONA VILLAGE

AND THE WINNERS ARE ... *For destinations resorts,* **BIG ISLAND 's South Kohala beauties define get-away-from-it-all luxury; Kaua'i's entries are second. For walking around** *resort trips,* **MAUI's Ka'anapali-Wailea combo can't be beaten, through many will prefer the over-the-top magnitude of Waikiki.**

Royal Hawaiian (The Pink Lady), Waikiki, Oahu; Marriott Kalapaki Bay, Kauai

24. INSPIRING CHURCHES and HOLY PLACES
Location, location, location—a wide range of religions have erected dramatic edifices.

Huialoha Church, Maui

KAUA'I

WAIOLI HUI'IA CHURCH
Tropical-green painted woodframe is an icon for the best of the Hawaii's missionary period.

88 HOLY PLACES OF KOBO DAISHI
Japanese shrines on a Kalaheo hillside promise to free all respectful visitors from original sin.

KAUA'I'S HINDU MONASTERY
Stop on the way from Wailua to Mount Waialeale to see the peaceful beginnings of what is planned to be a monumental monastery.

Worth a Look: ST. RAPHAEL'S CATHOLIC CHURCH (Koloa)

OAHU

BYODO IN-VALLEY OF THE TEMPLES
A lagoon reflects a storybook Buddhist temple, set below the vertical wall of the Ko'olau Range; on Windward side, near Kaneohe.

PUNCHBOWL (NATIONAL MEMORIAL CEMETERY OF THE PACIFIC)
The green crater above Honolulu is adorned with the markers of military veterans, and by a huge memorial mural and tribute to the unknown soldiers.

MORMON TEMPLE
A surreal vision on a gardenscaped hill above a new (2005) visitors center, close to the Polynesian Cultural Center.

ROYAL MAUSOLEUM
The Nu'uanu Valley resting place for most Hawaiian royalty and many historic figures. Presided over by the same family since the time of Kamehameha.

Worth a Look: KAWAIAHAO CHURCH (Honolulu)

MAUI

HUIALOHA CHURCH
The setting—on a rugged ocean cove near Kaupo on the remote south coast—makes this weather-beaten chapel a jewel.

ST. AUGUSTINE SHRINE-ST. GABRIEL CHURCH
Few visitors pull off the Hana Highway in Wailua (near Keanae) to see these sweet churches, surrounded by taro fields and framed by peaks.

`IHI'IHIOLEHOWAONA KAUA CHURCH
Off the Hana Highway in Keanae, an accent point in a field below a tropical mountainscape.

KIPAHULU CHURCH
Head past Hana and the national park to the forlorn, beautiful resting place of Charles Lindbergh, the most famous man of his day.

KEAWALAI CHURCH
Makena Landing's coral-rock church dates from 1832 and is the starting point for a pleasant beach path to the Maui Prince Beach.

KAULANAPUEO CHURCH
Serene spot in Huelo is a short side trip from the Hana Highway.

JODO MISSION
Only the West Maui Mountains could be a suitable backdrop for the enormous bronze Buddha in north Lahaina.

Worth a Look: FRANCIS XAVIER MISSION (Kahakuloa Village), ST. JOSEPH CHURCH (Kaupo), CHURCH OF THE HOLY GHOST (Kula)

BIG ISLAND

PAINTED CHURCH
Father Velge's tropics-inspired murals date from 1898. Add on big view of Kealakekua Bay.

MOKUAIKAUE CHURCH
Asa Thurston, leader of Hawaii's first missionaries of 1820, designed this coral-rock, breeze-cooled church in Kailua.

WOOD VALLEY TEMPLE
Modest structure is surrounded by lush forest. Dedicated by the Dali Lama in 1980.

AND THE WINNER IS ... Visitors can devote the whole photo album to MAUI's beautifully situated churches. Oahu's selections will also wow.

Painted Church, Big Island; 88 Holy Places of Kobo Diashi, Kauai; Keanae's church

25. SCENIC DRIVES
Yeah, there are traffic jams in Hawaii, but also many wandering highways worthy of a car commercial.

Kalalau Valley, Kauai

KAUA'I
NORTH SHORE (KEALIA TO KE'E BEACH)
The pasturelands and blue-water views of Kilauea give way to jungled, narrow roads and the Edenlike terminus at the Kalalau Trail. Plenty of beaches along the way.

WAIMEA CANYON
Several-thousand feet deep and 12 miles long, this pink-rock canyon rates with the best of the American Southwest—and it ends with a look over the edge to green Kalalau Valley.

Worth a Look: WEST SIDE TO POLIHALE BEACH

OAHU
WINDWARD PALI-H-3 FREEWAY
The view is already amazing as you come around the Waimanalo Coast. But hang onto your hat as the freeway rises and punches through the cliffs of the Ko'olau Range.

NORTH SHORE FROM LAIE TO MOLOKULIA COAST
Beach scene of the North Shore gets down-right rural as the highway follows the Waianae Range as it dives to the sea at road's end.

Worth a Look: WAIANAE COAST TO YOKOHAMA BAY

MAUI
HANA HIGHWAY-NU'U BAY SOUTH COAST
With waterfalls, one-lane bridges, and an explosion of greenery, the Hana Highway needs no introduction. But for the kicker, follow it around the desertlike, wild south shore, where big Haleakala rises inland.

HALEAKALA NATIONAL PARK-KULA UPCOUNTRY
World's highest-rising highway switchbacks get you to top-of-the-world views of the crater. Then drop down for the pastoral delights of Kula, at 4,000 feet.

KAHAKULOA VILLAGE-NORTH COAST
Follow the north Maui bluffs and seascapes, then grip the wheel as the road narrows to a lane and drops through a village valley.

BIG ISLAND
HAWAII VOLCANOES NATIONAL PARK
A rain forest is on one side of the park entrance, a lava wasteland with Mauna Loa views is on the other. And these are just a lead

up to a 10-mile crater rim drive, followed by a big descent to the coast, where new lava hits the ocean.

KEHENA-POHOIKI SCENIC COAST

The Puna Coast is Hawaii's sleeper: Tropics, fresh lava, natural, hot pools. Try a weekday for most serene viewing.

HAMAKUA COAST FROM
HILO TO WAIPIO VALLEY

Take portions of the Old Mamalahoa Highway north from Hilo, in and out of green gorges and sugar plantation communities, ending at the spectacular Waipio Valley Overlook.

SADDLE ROAD-MAUNA KEA-MAUNA LOA

A partially potholed two-laner cleaves the lava battlefield between Hawaii's mammoth mountains. Take a run up Mauna Loa and Mauna Kea for the full effect.

Worth a Look: KOHALA TO WAIMEA AND HAWI

AND THE WINNERS ARE ... Seamlessly scenic **KAUA'I** just can't be second best, so call it a co-winner with the wide-open, weird panoramas of the **BIG ISLAND**. More traffic on Maui and Oahu take them from contention for tops.

Mauna Kea observatories, Big Island; Hana Highway, Maui; Kehena-Pohoiki Scenic Drive, Big Island

26. PICNIC PARKS

Get out of the car and relax: A seaside table awaits in the shade of a swaying palm, or let birds serenade your table in the forest.

KAUA'I

KOKE'E STATE PARK
The great meadow between the canyon and the Napali is a forested respite, though wild chickens make a fuss for scraps.

LYDGATE PARK
Lots of pavilions, big playsets, and man-made ocean pool. Best family beach park in Hawaii.

ANINI BEACH
Find a spot along two miles of reef-protected shore, or hold down a table in the nicely treed park.

SALT POND BEACH PARK
A west side oasis, with good swimming and wistful palms.

KEALIA BEACH PARK
Surfer's action beach near Kapa'a was given a facelift in 2007—new pavilions and a paved shoreline path.

Worth a Look: POLIHALE STATE PARK (west side), POLIHALE, KUKUI TRAIL LOOKOUTS (Waimea Canyon), KUKUIOLONO PARK PAVILION (Kalaheo), KUKUIULA BAY (Prince Kuhio)

OAHU

KAILUA BEACH PARK
Rolling green backshore, dreamy offshore views, and excellent ocean sports and strolling. Popularity is the only drawback.

KOKOLOLIO BEACH PARK
Rolling lawns and pretty beach, just south of Polynesian Cultural Center in Laie.

POKAI BEACH PARK
Rough Waianae yields this scenic jewel, featuring a heiau on the point, protected swimming, and mauka views—a locals' favorite.

KUALOA REGIONAL PARK
Mokoli'i Island (Chinaman's Hat) lies fetchingly offshore, while the Ko'olaus rise inland from this large greenspace on the Windward Coast.

KAPIOLANI PARK
A huge city park lies beneath Diamond Head. Sweet beaches, communty sports, and events are a walk from Waikiki hotels.

Worth a Look: DOLE VISITORS CENTER (Wahiawa), KAIONA BEACH PARK (Waimanalo), KAIONA BEACH PARK (Kahala)

MAUI

WAIANAPANAPA STATE PARK
Located just as the Hana Highway comes out of the rain forest. Swimming, hiking, and lazing about are all possible. Try campside tables on the bluff just above the ocean.

KAMAOLE III BEACH PARK
The better of Kihei's three beach parks. Kihei's commerce gives it a slight downgrade, but the grass knolls and sandy beach are tops.

KAUMAHINA STATE WAYSIDE
Hana Highway's rest stop was given an ovehaul in 2006.

LAUNIUPOKO BEACH PARK
Good swimming and artfully placed palms, with an inland view of yawning valleys. Will improve when a planned bypass road eases traffic.

KEPANIWAI HERITAGE GARDENS
Take a break at the gateway to Iao Valley.

Salt Pond Beach Park, Kauai

Kualoa Regional Park, Oahu

Worth a Look: KAHEKILI BEACH PARK
(Ka'anapali), HONOKOWAI BEACH PARK
(Kapalua), RICE PARK (Kula), POLI POLI
SPRINGS STATE PARK (Kula Forest Reserve),
WAIHE'E BEACH PARK (Windward)

BIG ISLAND

PU'UHONUA BEACH PARK
    Tables under palms along a coastal path, next
    to the national park. Whale watch or take a
    dip in one of the lava seapools
HOLOHOLOKAI BEACH PARK
    Oasis between Puako and the Mauna Lani-
    Fairmont resorts in South Kohala. Combine
    lunch with a walk to the petroglyph field.
KAPA'A BEACH PARK
    A small pavilion above a wave-bashed shore
    is the perfect place to take a break in north
    Kohala.
PU'UOPELU-MANA HALE (PARKER RANCH)
    Pastoral pond-side setting is the best place to
    pull off the road in Waimea.

MACKENZIE STATE PARK
    A huge ironwood forest on the Puna Coast.
KALOPA STATE PARK
    Beautifully landscaped grounds and a variety
    of hiking trails grace this park, set at 2,000
    feet, just south of Honoka'a on the Hamakua
    Coast.

Worth a Look: HAPUNA STATE BEACH (South
Kohala, needs work), KOLEKOLE BEACH PARK
(Hamakua Coast), KEOKEA BEACH PARK
(Kohala), RICHARDSON OCEAN PARK (Hilo),
WAILUA RIVER STATE RECREATION AREA (Hilo),
ONEKAHAKAHA BEACH PARK (Hilo), MANUKA
STATE PARK (South Kona)

**AND THE WINNERS ARE ... Among beach parks,
give the edge to MAUI, but the Big Island has
an attractive variety, and Oahu and Kaua'i have
winners. Among forest and mountain parks, the
BIG ISLAND wins, but inshore parks of Kaua'i
and Maui are good choices.**

27. TROPICAL RIDGES AND PEAKS
*Look down to the sea from those scalloped, towering ridgelines—
the emerald escarpments that say "Hawaii."*

Kalalau Trail, Kauai

KAUA'I

KALALAU TRAIL (NAPALI COAST)
The famous trail hangs high on the majestic cliffs of the island's roadless northwest quadrant. Don't plan on day hiking the full 11 miles to Kalalau Valley.

AWA'AWAPUHI-NUALOLO TRAILS
The daylong loop trek down to the tip of a Napali precipice is to ridge hikes what the Eiffel is to towers and the Golden Gate is to bridges. Some of the precipices will make hikers gasp.

PIHEA TRAIL TO KILOHANA OVERLOOK
Over three-plus miles you go from the narrow rim of Kalalau Valley, on a boardwalk across the world's highest swamp, to a platform several thousand feet above Hanalei Bay. What the?!

KUILAU RIDGE TRAIL
Only a few miles long, the trail squiggles above a wealth of greenery in the interior near Mount Waialeale.

OKOLEHAO TRAIL
A four-mile, 1,200 foot scamper up a flora-rich stand-alone ridge separating the Hanalei and Waioli valleys.

POWERLINE TRAIL
Though not along a precipice, this 13-mile, one-way route goes between two mountain ranges across the interior of Kaua'i.

SLEEPING GIANT (NOUNOU FOREST RESERVE)
Three different trailheads are available to climb to the narrow top of this Coconut Coast landmark.

Worth a Look: KAHILI RIDGE (near Poipu turnoff), POLIHALE AND MILOLI'I RIDGES (Waimea Canyon)

OAHU

MOUNT OLYMPUS
The Wa'ahila Ridge Trail starts high and ratchets higher—almost 2,000 feet over 3.5 miles to a view of everywhere. The narrow terminus is on the edge of the vertical Ko'olau Range.

OLOMANA RIDGE
The triple-peaked dragon's back stands on the windward side. A media darling (N.Y. Times, etc.), the Olomana is not for beginners, cranking up 1,600 feet over two miles to a very skinny ridgeback.

KEALIA TRAIL-KUAOKALA TRAIL
Get the sensation of hang gliding on the switchbacks up the Waianae cliffs on the wild Mokuleia Coast.

KULIOUNOU RIDGE TRAIL
Lack of notoriety is an asset for this 5-mile roundtrip, 1,800-foot ascent of the southern Ko'olaus, above sunny Hawaii Kai.

WAIANAE KAI TRAIL TO MT. KA'ALA
Obscure parking and degree of difficulty keep this classic trek off the top of the list. An 8.5-mile roundtrip jaunt with more than 3,500 feet of elevation reaches the ethereal bog atop Oahu's highest peak.

WILIWILINUI RIDGE
Nice parking in a ritzy neighborhood transitions to a ridge road, and finally to a trail of ramps and benches to the top—three miles and 1,700 feet above your car.

Worth a Look: HAWAIILOA RIDGE TRAIL (Hawaiian driver's license required), STAIRWAY TO HEAVEN-HAIKU STAIRS (no lawful access), KOLOA RIDGE (Laie); MAU'UMAE RIDGE TRAIL (Honolulu),

MAUI

IAO VALLEY TABLELANDS
A short scramble (1.5 miles, roundtrip, and 250 feet) past the Iao Needle State Park viewing pavilion is Maui's best tropical mauka view. A narrow ridge lies between the Wall of Tears and the Kapilau Ridge, and gives a big view out the valley to the sea.

KAUPO TRAIL
A monster of a hike—14 miles and nearly 6,000 feet—up the forested south face of Haleakala and into the arid crater of the national park.

WAIHE'E RIDGE
A beautifully built and scenic trail to an interior vista, but it ends at a place where you really want to keep going—a roundtrip of 4.75 miles and 1,500 feet.

Worth a Look: WAIKALAI PLATEAU AND EKE CRATER TRAILS (north Maui), KAPILAU RIDGE (Wailuku)

BIG ISLAND

HONOKANE NUI, POLOLU VALLEY
Pololu is the bookend valley to Waipio, at road's end on the northwest side of the island. You drop into and out of several valleys, with 400-foot ridges in between. Old ruins are hidden in snarls of greenery.

MULIWAI TRAIL
Walk or take an SUV down to photogenic Waipio Beach and then up the Muliwai Trail, gateway to the Big Island's lush backcountry.

AINAPO TRAIL
The long way up Mauna Loa, through a forested birdland on the south slope. Don't plan on seeing other hikers—the trail covers 20 miles and climbs more than 10,000 feet.

Worth a Look: BAMBOO ALTAR FROM WHITE ROAD (Waimea, access problem.)

AND THE WINNER IS ... KAUA'I has had a few more million years to erode into the hiker's tropical fantasyland it is today. Given its urbanization, Oahu has a surprising number of good hikes up the ridges of the Ko'olau Mountains.

Olomana Ridge, Oahu

28. WATERFALLS
Scenic overlooks and longer hikes to where all that rain gathers and drops in white ribbons and cascades.

KAUA'I
WAIALEALE BLUE HOLE
A short hike (a couple miles, if you make a several-mile drive on a dirt road) leads to the 'birthplace of all waters.' A high-altitude swamp lies behind the peak, sending about a half-dozen ribbony falls down its vertical face.
HANAKAPIAI FALLS
Go two miles on the famous Kalalau Trail, and then another tough two up a jungle gorge to a classic 300-foot waterfall.
WAIOLI VALLEY
No public trails lead in, but the view from Hanalei after the rains is unforgettable.
WAILUA FALLS
Tour buses hammer the overlook for this *Fantasy Island* opening shot, but not the steep trail down to a river crossing and the pool at the bottom. (Never attempt during high water.)
WAIPO'O FALLS
The trail leads to the top of this red-dirt Waimea Canyon beauty, so you have to save the photo ops for scenic viewpoints across the canyon.

Worth a Look: KIPU FALLS (Kipu), HO'OPI'I FALLS (Kapa'a)

OAHU
LAIE FALLS
A lesser-known, 6-mile, 1,400-foot hike, to a hidden 30–foot falls, pool, and second cascade.
WAIMANO FALLS
Head into the Ko'olau Mountains above suburban Honolulu to find a cascade into bed-rock—a 3.25-mile, 725-foot elevation hike.
MANOA FALLS
Popularity is the only drawback for this scamper through fanciful greenery next to Lyon Arboretum to a classic jungle falls.
MAUNAWILI FALLS
A mini-adventure up a stream valley in the Ko'olaus on the Windward side.
LIKEKE FALLS
The best-kept secret of among Oahu falls hikes, sitting below the Nu'uanu Pali.

Wailua Falls, Kauai

MAUI

FALLS AT MAKAHIKU-WAIMOKU FALLS
Best falls hike in Hawaii—4.25 miles and an 850-foot climb over bridges and through a bamboo forest. It's at the end of the Hana Highway and above the Pools of Oheo.

WALL OF TEARS
A vertical cliff above Iao Needle gets streaked with white falls. You don't get close, but you need distance to take it all in.

POOLS OF OHEO
At "journeys end" for Hana Highway day-trippers, this portion of Haleakala National Park can be a zoo. But when swimming is bad due to rains, the cascades are pumping.

TWIN FALLS
A series of cascades and pools at the beginning of the Hana Highway.

HANA HIGHWAY
Dozens of falls feed the streams along this world-famous scenic drive. Access can be a problem, but the scenic drive is fab.

ALELELE FALLS
Tucked away in the newest (undeveloped) portion of Haleakala National Park. Unsigned and off a narrow road; the walk is short.

BIG ISLAND

BOILING POTS-WAILUKU RIVER STATE PARK
A short drop down from a scenic viewpoint leads to bedrock tabletops, pools, and a wide falls. Stay away in high water—these pots do boil—but chill out in the sun at this close-to-Hilo getaway.

AKAKA FALLS STATE PARK
On the tour bus circuit, yes. But you also get Kahuna Falls on a short jungle loop trail. Akaka is a long, wide freefall.

KALUAHINE FALLS, WAIPIO VALLEY
Walk by the top on the way down, then scramble up the beach at the bottom and look straight up at it.

RAINBOW FALLS
Tour buses create visual noise, but hang around for a while at the overlook. The kicker is the short trail to bedrock pools at the top.

KAPIOLOA FALLS
Hawaii Forest & Trail will guide you along historic ditches to this cliff-hanging beauty.

Worth a look: UMAUMA FALLS OVERLOOK (Hamakua Coast)

AND THE WINNER IS ... Give MAUI the edge, but Kaua'i and the Big Island score big, and Oahu has more trails that end at falls.

Kapioloa Falls, Big Island
(Trail may be closed due to
earthquake of 2006.)

29. RAIN FOREST & STREAM VALLEYS
An overwhelming profusion of greenery in all directions at arm's length.

Alakai Swamp, Kauai

KAUA'I

ALAKAI SWAMP
A boardwalk aids the way on Hawaii's best rain forest walk. Slow down and take a look around—and then march to the 4,000-foot-high overlook at the edge of the swamp looking down at Hanalei Bay.

HANALEI RIVER
An unfriendly trailhead along an otherwise beautiful Hanalei River keeps people (but not weekend hunters) off this oh-wow route. The trail penetrates bamboo and hau thickets.

WAIMEA RIVER-MENEHUNE DITCH TRAIL
Same deal for this hike as above: odd trailhead access, but thrilling trail for the adventurous hiker. You cross an Indiana Jones-type footbridge.

WAIALEALE STREAM CONVERGENCE
Waialeale and saw-toothed sister ridges encircle a broad watershed, shaded by an overstory of Monkeypod trees.

OAHU

AHUPUA'A O KAHANA STATE PARK
You'll feel like you've been on a jungle expedition after completing a loop in this deep crease of the Ko'olau Range.

MAUNAWILI TRAIL
A willy-nilly contour along the base of the Ko'olaus on the Windward side, passing numerous streams and tangles of greenery.

MOANALUA VALLEY
The seven stone bridges of an old estate add a touch of fancy to an easy walk up a stream valley beginning in suburban Honolulu.

MAUI

SWINGING BRIDGES
Nothing like cable-and-plank bridges across a river to bring out the sense of adventure. This hike penetrates the 3,000-foot-deep Waihe'e Valley.

IAO STEAM, IAO VALLEY STATE PARK
Take this easy nature walk at the state park, or sign up for a tour at nearby Hawaii Nature Center

Worth a Look: LITTLE JURASSIC PARK (Hana Highway, access problem), OLOWALU VALLEY (sketchy trail)

BIG ISLAND

KAU FOREST AT LORENZO ROAD
A new and lesser-known trail near South Point skirts the mysterious forest of the newest portion of Hawaii Volcanoes National Park.

KAHAUALEA NATURAL AREA
Claustrophobia may set in as you wind through a rain forest in Puna, headed for a clearing and a view of the active volcano.

MAKA'ALA TREE FERN FOREST
A short, fairyland walk through the giant ferns, alongside the Ola'a Wilderness portion of the national park.

CRATER RIM TRAIL–HAWAII VOLCANOES NATIONAL PARK
One side of Kilauea Caldera is barren. The other is a bird-filled, magical ohia-and-tree-fern forest.

WAIPIO VALLEY TARO FIELDS
Most people head to the beach, but upriver leads to Old Hawaii taro fields, framed by the waterfall-laced valley walls.

AND THE WINNER IS ... Oddly enough the most-barren **BIG ISLAND** gets the overall vote, based on its green north and east. Kaua'i's wilds and Oahu's best are excellent; much of Maui's jungle forest doesn't have approved hiker access.

Kau Forest, Big Island; Swinging Bridges, Maui

30. EASY WALKS TO CLASSIC HAWAIIAN VISTAS
Places to get a faraway vista (and beat the crowd) just steps from the car.

KAUA'I

PIHEA OVERLOOK OF KALALAU VALLEY
Road's end at the top of Waimea Canyon is the beginning of a trail around the lip of Kalalau Valley.

HANALEI PIER
A set for many movies, the pier at Black Pot Beach is the focus of the surfer-locals beach scene. The view is across the bay to the ridge that was heralded in the folk song, *Puff the Magic Dragon.*

KE'E BEACH TO NAPALI VIEW
For heaven's sake, take a walk a few hundred feet from up the beach at road's end to see the profiles of the Napali stretching off into the distance.

KUKI'I POINT LIGHT-NININI POINT LIGHTHOUSE
With the Hoary Head rising above Nawiliwili Harbor, watch from either of these lighthouses as a cruise ship departs at sunset.

PU'U KA PELE
An unusual short trail past a phone installation gets you to the cinder cone hanging on the side of Waimea Canyon, where volcano goddess Pele left her footprint when leaving Kaua'i.

Worth a Look: PU'U HINAHINA LOOKOUT (Waimea Canyon), WAILUA RIVER-SLEEPING GIANT AT SMITHS TROPICAL PARADISE (Wailua)

OAHU

DIAMOND HEAD AND WAIKIKI FROM MAGIC ISLAND
The best of many places for the iconic postcard shot.

OLD PALI HIGHWAY-NU'UANU PALI LOOKOUT
Tour buses hammer the precipice where hundreds of Oahu warriors took a fall in 1795. For solitude, take a short walk down the old highway, which is being reclaimed by the jungle.

WAIANAE COAST FROM POKAI BEACH PARK HEIAU
The famous Oahu navigator, Pokai, set sail from this sacred spot.

WINDWARD SIDE FROM ABOVE MAKUPU'U LOOKOUT
Take a scamper up the hillside from the paved turnout for a more personal look at the romantic Ko'olau Range and the tiny islands off the Windward Coast.

Worth a Look: HONOLULU FROM SAND ISLAND, TANTALUS SUMMIT-PU'U UALAKA'A LOOKOUT (Honolulu), DANNY CAMPLIN OVERLOOK (Waimea Bay), KOLEKOLE PASS (Schofield Barracks)

MAUI

WHITE HILL-HALEAKALA VISITORS CENTER
These popular viewpoints atop the volcano live up to their reputation. Watch the light and weather change.

HALEAKALA FROM PU'U MANEONEO ABOVE NU'U BAY
A pastoral bluff on the remote coast of south Maui. The big Volcano rises 10,000 feet from the sweeping, lava seascape.

KUKUIPUKA HEIAU
Near the Waihe'e Ridge Trailhead is a short path to a green heiau platform that overlooks Kahului and the windward shore.

OLOWALU LANDING
This historical site features a variety of trees, marine life swimming by and a classic view of the valley inland.

Worth a Look: PU'U OLAI (Makena), FAGAN'S CROSS (Hana), QUEEN KA'AHUMANU BIRTHPLACE (Hana), LAHAINA SEAWALL

Hanalei Pier, Kauai

BIG ISLAND

MAUNA KEA SUMMIT

Drive (the last part four-wheel) to the .25-mile trail that leads to the tallest mountain in the world (measured from its base).

HILO FROM MOKU OLA (COCONUT ISLAND)

A footbridge leads to a tiny island with a palm tiara. Across the bay is Hilo Town, and rising in the sky to either side are Mauna Kea and Mauna Loa.

KILAUEA CALDERA FROM VOLCANO HOUSE

Far below, but in your face, is the signature view of Hawaii Volcanoes National Park.

MAUNA LOA OBSERVATORY

Drive up to 11,000 feet, where scientists measure world weather—with a view of Maui, Mauna Kea, and Hualalai Volcano like islands in the sky.

WAIPIO VALLEY LOOKOUT

Waterfall, river, beach, valley, and cliffs combine for a sum greater than the parts.

Worth a Look: PU'U HULUHULU (Saddle Road), POLOLU VALLEY LOOKOUT (North Kohala), KEALAKEKUA BAY FROM PALEMANO POINT (Ke'ei Village)

AND THE WINNER IS ... tough to determine, but go with KAUA'I. For short hikes to eye-candy, the other islands are close behind—Big Island, Maui, and Oahu, in that order.

Waipio Valley Lookout, Big Island; Olowalu Landing, Maui

31. DRY AND HIGH

The leeward sides have canyons with cacti und dwarf flora, and many of Hawaii's peaks are above the treeline: you'll be reminded of the American Southwest, only flouting in the Pacific Ocean.

KAUA'I

KUKUI TRAIL INTO WAIMEA CANYON
The trail drops 2,000 feet to the bottom of the canyon, passing orange rock tufted with greenery, wild goats, and giant century cacti.

HAELE'ELE RIDGE
One of several walks out—and down—the more arid Napali ridges, beginning off the road along the rim of Waimea Canyon.

KUMUWELA LOOKOUT-WAIPO'O FALLS
Okay, you start in a lush forest. But the culmination of the hike is a barren head of land above the depths of pink-walled Waimea Canyon.

OAHU

KOKO CRATER STAIRS
More than 1,000 railroad ties (part of a WWII-era tramway) ascend to the crater inland from Hanauma Bay.

DIAMOND HEAD
Put on your cowbell and join the ill-prepared herd, climbing to the top rim of Honolulu's landmark. Steps, tunnels, bunkers, and a spiral staircase are part of an oddball route.

Kukui Trail, Kauai

MAUI

HALEMANU'U TRAIL TO KO'OLAU GAP
Follow Haleakala's east rim to the point where a torrent of lava once spilled to form the Keanae peninsula along today's Hana Highway. Then switchback down a cliff into the valley of the volcano.

SLIDING SANDS TRAIL
The cover-shot trail in the park. Head into the huge open bowl, swirling with pink and yellow landforms and cinder cones.

SKYLINE TRAIL
This seldom used trail drops down the west face of Haleakala, giving up a big sea view, and ends in the Kula Forest Reserve.

LAHAINA PALI TRAILS
Big blue-water views on the leeward, arid slope of the West Maui Mountains.

Worth a Look: PAHIHI GULCH (south coast)

BIG ISLAND

LAKE WAIAU (MAUNA KEA ICE AGE NATURAL AREA RESERVE)
Make your own moon walk through rock formations leading to one of the world's highest alpine lakes at 13,000 feet—fed by a gradually melting permafrost under Mauna Kea's slopes.

MAUNA LOA NORTH PIT
The trail starts at the 11,000-foot-high observatory and ascends the round slope of the volcano's active zone.

PU'U O'O HORSE TRAIL
Begin at a jagged lava field on Saddle Road and walk onto the smooth lava and kipukas (small islands of spared trees) in the vast sweep between Mauna Loa and Mauna Kea.

HALEMAUMAU CRATER-KILAUEA CRATER
Kilauea Crater is a rumpled sheet of lava, about 4 miles across, and within it is Halemaumau, the house of fiery goddess Pele—which blew its cork in 1974 and still fumes.

Worth a Look: KA'AHA SHELTER-HILINA PALI KAU DESERT TRAIL (both Hawaii Volcanoes National Park)

AND THE WINNER IS ... The breadth of activity on the slopes of MAUI'S Haleakala make this island the overall choice, though some will argue for the Big Island.

Sliding Sands Trail, Haleakala National Park, Maui

32. BIRDWATCHING FORESTS
*Twitters and chirps from deep within native and
non-native forests. (See Whales & Wildlife, page 84, for seabirds.)*

KAUA'I
KOKE'E STATE PARK
Forests above the Waimea Canyon are rich in
bird life, including some of Hawaii's
endangered species. Lots of trails.

KUIA NATURAL AREA RESERVE
A bird zone is pocketed into the west side of
Koke'e Park, at the edge of Napali ridges.

KEAHUA ARBORETUM
Below Mount Waialale is a wide tableland,
crossed by several streams.

KAHILI PINE FOREST
Norfolk pines and leafy trees are pocketed
into the lowlands of Kahili Ridge, near Poipu.

LAPA PICNIC AREA
Contour Road follows the forests and streams
at the upper reaches of the west Napali ridges,
passing this picnic area.

Worth a Look: SPALDING MONUMENT (Kealia)

OAHU
HAWAII NATURE CENTER-KANEALOLE TRAIL
An easy walk from the Tantalus Trail system
above Honolulu, starting at the newly built
visitor center.

HAU'ULA FOREST RESERVE
Two trails loop the spur ridges of the Ko'olau
Range at the north end of Windward side.

KULIOUOU VALLEY
Short and sweet, this hike leads from Hawaii
Kai, in the southwest end of the Ko'olaus.

Worth a Look: AIEA LOOP TRAIL (Honolulu),
KAUNALA TRAIL (Pupukea, North Shore)

MAUI
**POLI POLI SPRINGS STATE PARK-
KULA FOREST RESERVE**
Plenty of action at this network of trails set at
6,000 feet above Kula, but well below the west
slopes of Haleakala. Redwoods anyone?

HOSMER GROVE NATURE TRAIL
Interpretive signs give beginning birders a
good start on this short loop at the entrance to
Haleakala National Park.

WAIHOU SPRINGS FOREST RESERVE
Go up Olinda Road from Makawao and
you'll find a quiet forested trail; Maui Bird
Conservation Center is nearby.

WAIKAMOI RIDGE NATURE TRAIL
One of the few places to get off into the forest
from the Hana Highway.

BIG ISLAND
KIPUKA PUAULU (BIRD PARK)
A kipuka is an "island" of vegetation surrounded by lava flows. This birdy one is at the
bottom of Mauna Loa Road, near the entrance
to Hawaii Volcanoes National Park.

CRATER RIM TRAIL-HALEMAUMAU TRAIL
Birdsong is the soundtrack in the ferny forests
on the wet side of Kilauea Crater, near Volcano
House.

WOOD VALLEY-KAU FOREST
The tranquil, green Ninole forests are a sharp
contrast to the lava downslopes of the Big
Island's east coast—near Pahala.

MANUKA STATE PARK
Native ohia, as well as other trees, mark the
way on a secluded loop at this park—about
midway between Kona and Hawaii Volcanoes
National Park.

KALOPA NATIVE FOREST STATE PARK
Short nature trails and longer forest reserve
loops give birders options. Kalopa is a
beautifully kept park, set at 2,000 feet at the
north end of the Hamakua Coast.

Worth a Look: PU'U WA'A WA'A (access limited,
above South Kohala), HAKALAU NATIONAL
WILDLIFE REFUGE (hard to get to, Mana Road),
LAVA TREES STATE MONUMENT (Puna)

**AND THE WINNER IS ... KAUA'I'S lush interior
puts it a beak ahead of the Big Island's rain- and
dry-land forests as best for birders. Maui is just
chirps away in third.**

Kalopa Native Forest State Park, Big Island

33. VOLCANO CRATERS AND LAVA
Technically, all Hawaiian hikes are in this category, but on these you'll know it for sure.

KAUA'I
PU'U WANAWANA CRATER

Hiding in plan sight in Poipu near the Hyatt is the cacti-covered cone of Kaua'i's last eruption—thousands of years ago.

OAHU
DIAMOND HEAD-KOKO CRATER

Lava is covered by dwarf vegetation, but from the top of these formations there's no doubt of their fiery origins.

MAUI
HALEAKALA NATIONAL PARK

The vast interior of the volcano is pocked with numerous cinder cones, dunes, and rock formations. Technically, Haleakala is not dormant, having erupted (best guess) within the last 300 to 500 years.

BIG ISLAND
PU'U O'O FLOWS

Volcanoes are unpredictable, but for more than 20 years this cone of Kilauea Volcano has been sending bursts and streams of lava into the sea, adding more than 800 acres of new land the island. You can drive 20 miles from the visitors center to take a look.

KILAUEA CALDERA

About ten miles in circumference, Kilauea is the centerpiece of Hawaii Volcanoes National Park. Drive around it, stopping at numerous lookouts and trails.

IKI CRATER

Iki is still steaming from its 1959 outburst. A popular loop trail transects this offshoot of Kilauea Caldera.

Iki Crater Trail, Hawaii Volcanoes National Park, Big Island

PU'U HULUHULU-CHAIN OF CRATERS
   The reward for hiking to this little
   cone is a distant view of active Pu'u
   O'o; a half-dozen craters along
   a drive tell the story of Kilauea's
   east rift, with flows dating from the
   1960s.

THURSTON LAVA TUBE
   Walk through a huge lava tube that
   lies close to the road in a tree-fern
   forest. The parked tour buses mark
   the spot.

HALEMAUMAU CRATER
   On the desolate west side of Kilauea
   Caldera is Pele's House, a fuming
   crater that was a lake of lava in
   1924, and erupted most recently in
   1974.

KALAPANA LAVA BAY
   Kilauea's recent outburst destroyed
   200 homes, ancient heiaus, two
   county parks, and filled this bay
   with pahoehoe (smooth) lava.

**AND THE WINNER IS ... Did anybody
guess BIG ISLAND?**

Puu Oo, Big Island; Koko Crater, Oahu

34. BICYCLE TOURING & MOUNTAIN BIKING

KAUA'I
Road Touring
WAILUA TO ANAHOLA BIKE PATH
You'll need wheels that can handle patches of unpavement, but this coastal ride-around route of nearly 20 miles is one of Hawaii's best, extending along the resorts and wild areas of the Coconut Coast.

HIGHWAY 50 ANAHOLA TO PRINCEVILLE
The highway from the end of the bike path after Kealia, and is bike friendly for the next 18 miles to Princeville. County lanes provide scenic side trips, which loop back to the highway.

FROM LIHUE TO POIPU
A side route through Nawiliwili Harbor and Kipu is a rural road ride along Hoary Head Ridge. Narrow highway sections and traffic after Poipu make highways iffy, with no options to get around.

Be Aware: The pretty north shore ride from Princeville through Hanalei to the end of the road at the beginning of the Kalalau Trail has no shoulder in most places and is dangerous for road bikes.

Mountain Biking
POWERLINE TRAIL
A 13-mile jaunt through the center of the island to Princeville to Kapa'a is one of Hawaii's best.

KEAHUA ARBORETUM
Miles of unpaved-and-puddled roads lead to Waialeale's Blue Hole (wettest spot on earth) as well as a fun ride over Kuilau Ridge.

NAPALI WEST RIDGES
As you drive up Waimea Canyon, a half-dozen different state forest roads lead out and down Napali's lesser-known ridgetops. Rides are about 12 miles roundtrip and drop an average of 1,500 feet.

KOKE'E STATE PARK
At the top of Waimea Canyon is a network of unpaved, birdland forest roads, as well as Contour Road, which crosses the Napali rides mentioned above.

OAHU
Road Touring
NORTH SHORE BIKE PATH,
KAMEHAMEHA HIGHWAY
A bike path and side lane front the beach for miles from Pupukea to beyond Sunset Beach. Although you need to watch for traffic, King Kamehameha Highway around the North Shore is bikeable—as is the Farrington Highway along the Mokuleia Coast.

WAIKIKI
Getting around Oahu's fabled grid of resorts—from Ala Moana Beach Park to Kapiolani Park below Diamond Head, is faster on two wheels than in a car. Places rent bikes by the week.

Mountain Biking
Not the best island for mountain biking.

MAUI
Road Touring
HALEAKALA DOWNHILL
Hoards of people get a big thrill coasting 38 miles down the twisting volcano highway.

KAHULUI TO PAIA
A bike path and safe byways make this a good get-around route, but probably not all that interesting for vacationers.

KULA HIGHWAY
The upcountry cruise from Makaweo to Ulupalakua Ranch sees road bikes. Adventure cyclists can also continue along the lonely south coast.

John Alford's Bike Hawaii, Oahu

Lower slopes of Haleakala, Maui

Be Aware: Hana Highway is dangerous on a bike. Other trans-island roads have lots of car traffic. The road around the north side is too narrow to hold bikes and cars.

Mountain Biking
KULA FOREST RESERVE
The forest roads and trails, which include Poli Poli Springs State Park are a fun ride. Skyline Trail, which descends Haleakala, is a lot better than taking the highway down, but few take this route.

BIG ISLAND
HIGHWAY NORTH FROM KAILUA KONA
Ironman Triathlon cyclists take the wide shoulder of Queen Ka'ahumanu Highway north of Kailua through sun-scorched, windblown, endless fields of jagged lava. You can too!
HAMAKUA HIGHWAY
A scenic workout for road cyclists that includes miles-long side trips on the Old Mamalahoa Highway. Traffic a concern, but not a problem.
HAWAII VOLCANOES NATIONAL PARK
Roads within the park, including Crater Rim Drive and the pump up to Mauna Loa Lookout, are bike friendly. You'll also find smooth sailing from Hilo to the park headquarters, and from there down the east side to South Point.

Be Aware: The highway south from Kona to Manuka State Park, a distance of about 30 miles, is dangerous due to lack of shoulder—the missing segment in an otherwise bike-friendly island circumnavigation. Also (!) avoid Highway 190, the Mamalahoa highway from Kona to Waimea, with crazy drivers and no shoulders.

Mountain Biking
MANA ROAD
A 4WD road takes a high contour around Mauna Kea, one of the best rides in Hawaii.
MUD LANE – PU'UHUE ROAD
These dirt tracks drop from the green Kohala Mountains. Mud is on the Waipio Valley side, Pu'uhue Road drops to the pasturelands on the west side.
ROAD TO THE SEA
You drop a bumpy 2,000 feet over 7 miles to a remote, rough coast on the west side, way south of Kona.
BEACH ROAD – OLD PUNA TRAIL
A long adventure along the coast south of Hilo.
KULANI TRAILS
A network of tropical forest reserve roads off the main highway from Hilo to Hawaii Volcanoes National Park create an under-explored mountain biking park.
WAIKEA TREE PLANTING ROAD
Wide track goes 12 miles from the moonscape off Saddle Road (between Mauna Kea and Mauna Loa) to lush Stainback Highway out of Hilo, and the Kulani Trails mentioned about.

AND THE WINNERS ARE ... For *road bike touring* the **BIG ISLAND is the best, followed by Kaua'i. For tooling around on a bike, Oahu's North Shore and Waikiki make a lot of sense, as does Kauai's Coconut Coast, Hanalei Town, and Poipu Beach You can also explore South Kohala resorts around Puako comfortably on a bike.**

Mountain biking **is a toss up. KAUA'I is hard to beat and all but one of the best rides don't require a car shuttle. On the BIG ISLAND, adventure bikers can really get into the hinterlands. Works best if you have a support vehicle.**

Wahine paniolo, Waimea rodeo, Kauai

35. HORSEBACK RIDING

KAUA'I

NORTH SHORE

Silver Falls Ranch and Princeville Ranch Stables have rides on vast ranches on the green upslopes, with blue-water views and the green ridges of Kaua'i's interior rising above.

EAST SIDE

Esprit de Corps Riding Academy's trails swerve through a lush valley that leads toward Mount Waialeale.

SOUTH SHORE

CJM Country Stable's riders go from near the Hyatt to the open, drier lands of Mahaulepu Beach with distinctive Hoary Head Ridge as a backdrop.

OAHU

WINDWARD

Kualoa Ranch has lots of green, mountainous tropical acreage that has welcomed numerous Hollywood movie crews.

NORTH SHORE

Happy Trails Hawaii will take you on an affordable ride in the green forests above fabled surfing beaches.

MAUI

HALEAKALA

Haleakala on Horseback goes to cabins within the desertlike crater of the national park. Adventures on Horseback and Horse Whisperer are out of the cowboy town on Makawao, off the main road up to Haleakala. Down the contour highway in Kula is Pony Express Tours, and around the mountain near Hana is Ohio Stables. Makena Stables is close to Wailea, and rides up toward Ulupalakua Ranch.

NORTH MAUI

Ironwood Ranch rides into the countryside above Kapalua on the west side, while venerable Mendes Ranch takes in the coastal area by the bird sanctuary islands on Maui's windward side.

BIG ISLAND

WAIMEA

Thousands of acres of Parker Ranch and the high pastures between Mauna Kea and the North Kohala Mountains are the setting for several outfitters, includng Ainahou Ranch, Dahana Ranch, Kohala Na'alapa Stables, and Paniolo Adventures.

WAIPIO VALLEY

See the striking, historic valley on horseback courtesy of Waipio on Horseback or Waipio Ridge Stables.

CJM Stables, Kauai

SOUTH KOHALA
Mauna Kea Beach Stables provides coastal experience.

KEALIA RANCH
This huge ranch south of Kona will open a whole new world beneath Mauna Loa.

KAPAPALA RANCH
Huge acreage south of Hawaii Volcano National Park takes in the east side of Mauna Loa.

AND THE WINNERS ARE ... Truth is you can get an excellent trail ride on all the islands. But KAUA'I, MAUI, and the BIG ISLAND offer many choices and a range of beautiful scenery. It's really a toss-up among those three.

Hawaiian paniolos were herding cattle decades before the cowboys of the American West. Today's riders compete in professional rodeo tours (a Hawaiian was the West's first champ in the 1800s).

Wild horse, Waipio Valley, Big Island

Kapalua, Maui

36. GOLF

SELECTED COURSES

KAUAI
> Kauai Lagoons Golf Course 241-6000
> Grove Farm Golf Course at Puakea
> 245-8756
> Kiahuna Golf Club, Poipu 742-9595
> Kukuiolono Golf Course, Kalaheo
> 332-9151
> Poipu Bay Resort Golf Course
> 800-858-6300
> Princeville Golf Club 800-826-1105
> Wailua Golf Club 241-6666

OAHU
> Ala Wai Golf Course 733-7387
> Hawaii Country Club, Waihiawa 621-5654
> Hawaii Kai Championship Golf Course
> 395-2358
> Hawi Prince Golf Club, Ewa 944-4567
> Kapolei Golf Course 674-2227
> Ko Olina Golf Club 676-5300
> Ko'olau Golf Course, Windward 236-4653
> Luana Hills Country Club, Windward
> 262-2139
> Makaha Resort Gold Club 695-7519
> Moanalua Golf Club 839-2311
> Turtle Bay Resort, Palmer Course 293-8574

MAUI
> Dunes at Maui Lani 873-0422
> Ka'anapali Tournament Golf Course
> 661-3691
> Kapalua Plantation Golf Course
> 877-527-2582
> Also The Bay and The Village courses
> Makena Golf Club, North & South
> 879-3344
> Maui Country Club 877-0616
> Pukalani Country Club 572-1314
> Waiehu Municipal Golf Course 270-7400
> Wailea Golf Clubs, Blue Course 871-5155
> Gold and Emerald courses 875-7450

BIG ISLAND
> Hapuna Golf Course 880-3000
> Hilton Waikoloa Seaside 886-1234
> Big Island Country Club 325-5044
> Francis H. I'i Brown (Mauna Lani)
> North & South Courses 885-6655
> Waikoloa Beach Course 886-6060
> Waikoloa Kings' Course 886-7888
> Waimea Country Club 885-8777
> Kona Country Club 322-2595
> Makalei Hawaii Club 325-6625
> Hamakua Country Club 775-7244
> Sea Mountain Golf Course 928-6222
> Volcano Country Club 967-7331

KAUA'I

Kaua'i has "only" nine golf courses, but among them is Poipu Bay Golf Club, home to PGA's Grand Slam. Kukuiolono and Wailua are two of Hawaii's best municipal courses. Princeville's two courses have received acclaim in golfing publications.

OAHU

Oahu has 31 public and semi-private courses—three of which are rated among the state's top ten: Makaha Resort, Coral Creek, and Ko'olau Golf Course.

MAUI

Among Maui's 16 courses are the Kapalua Plantation, which hosts the Mercedes Championship that opens the PGA season in January and is rated in Hawaii's top ten. The Wailea Golf course is home to the Senior Skins Game, and Makena North is top-ten pick among pros. On the windward side, the Waiehu Municipal course is a beautiful bargain.

BIG ISLAND

The Mauna Kea, designed by Arnold Palmer, and the Hualalai, designed by Jack Nicklaus and home to PGA events, are two of the Big Island's 19 courses. The Kona Country Club is rated among the state's ten best.

AND THE WINNER IS ... Golfers will not be disappointed on any island, but MAUI gets the nod as overall best, based on courses, aesthetics, and weather. The Big Island nudges Oahu for second, though many golfers would disagree. That leaves fourth for Kaua'i, which has some of the best golfing in the world.

Wailua Golf Club, Kauai

Orchid; Kekaha Kai State Park, Lapakahi State Park, Big Island; Napali Coast, Kauai

WikiWiki Phonebook

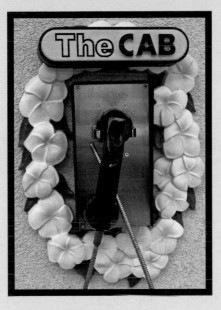

WikiWiki (QuickQuick)
It's faster than a speeding Internet!
Able to talk story with real Hawaiians with the push of buttons!
(All area codes are 808 unless otherwise noted)

Visitor Information

KAUAI
Kaua'i Visitors Bureau 245-3971, 800-262-1400
Kaua'i Heritage Center of Hawaiian Culture & Arts
821-2070
Garden Island Arts Council, Lihue 246-4561
Ka'ie'ie Foundation, perpetuating Hawaiian culture
821-2070
Chamber of Commerce 245-7363
Hawaii Visitor and Conventions Bureau 800-464-2924
Mayor's Office 241-6300
Public Libraries, Lihue 241-3222
Weather 245-6001
Wind and Surf Conditions 245-3564, 245-6001
Hawaiian Waters report 245-3564, 335-3720

OAHU
Oahu Visitors Bureau 877-525-6248
Haleiwa Main Street 637-4558
Office of Hawaiian Affairs 594-1888
Surf Reports 596-7873 (SURF)
Weather 973-4380
Hawaii Tourism Authority, Honolulu 973-2255

MAUI
Maui Visitors Bureau 800-525-6284, 244-3530
Maui Chamber of Commerce 871-7711
Destination Lanai 800-947-4774, 565-7600
Molokai Visitors Association 800-800-6367, 553-3876
Weather forecast 877-5111, 877-3477
    Lanai, 565-6033; Molokai 552-2477
Hawaiian Natural History Association 985-6051
Lahaina Restoration Foundation 661-3262
Malama Kahakai (coastal preservation) 579-9802
Maui Arts & Cultural Center 242-2787
Maui Historical Society 244-3326
Maui Museums Association 871-8058
Maui Tomorrow 877-2462, 572-8331
The Nature Conservancy 572-7849
Sierra Club 579-9802, 573-3454; hikes 573-4147

BIG ISLAND
Big Island Visitors Bureau 800-648-2441,
    Hilo 961-5797, Kona 886-1655
Destination Kona Coast 322-6809, 327-9373
Destination Hilo 935-5294
Mauna Kea Management Office, University of Hawaii,
    Hilo 944-0734
Weather, island-wide 961-5582, Hilo, 935-8555

Accommodations
C = Cheap, under $100
M = Moderate, $100 to $200
P = Pricey, $200 and up
**All listings are recommended;
boldfaced listings are preferred**

KAUAI
NORTH SHORE (KILAUEA, PRINCEVILLE, HANALEI)
Aloha Sunrise Inn, Kilauea (cottages) (M)
    888 828 1000, 828-1100
Anini Aloha Properties (Agent) (M-P) 800-323-4450
Hanalei Bay Resort, Princeville (Resort) (M-P)
    800-922-7866
Hanalei Colony Resort, Haena (Hotel) (P)
    800-628-3004
**Hanalei North Shore Properties (Roberta Haas,
    Agent) (M-P) 800-488-3336, 826-9622**
Oceanfront Realty (Agent) (C-P)
    800-222-5541, 826-6585
**Princeville Resort (Resort) (P)
    800-782-9488, 826-9644**

COCONUT COAST (KAPA'A, WAILUA. LIHUE)
Aloha Beach Resort (Resort), Wailua (M-P)
    888-823-5111
Alohilani (B&B) (C) 800-533-9316
Garden Island Properties (Agent) (C-P) 800-801-0378
Islander on the Beach (Hotel) (C-M) 800-847-7417
Kauai Palms Hotel, Lihue (C) 246-0908
Kauai Coast Resort, Wailua (P)
    877-977-4355, 822-3441
Makana Crest (B&B) (C) 245-6500
Island Rentals (Agent) (C-M) 822-4899
Plantation Hale (Condos)(M) 800-775-4253
Pono Kai (Condos) (M-P) 800-535-0085, 822-9831
Rainbow's End (B&B cottage) (C-M)
    961-3833, 966-4663
Sleeping Giant Realty (Agent) (C-M) 800-247-8831
Treehouse, Kapa'a (cottage) (C) 822-7681
Garden Island Inn (Hotel), Lihue (C-M) 800-648-0154
Hilton Kauai Beach Resort (M-P)
    800-445-8667, 245-1955

POIPU BEACH. WEST SIDE
Gloria's Spouting Horn (B&B) (P) 742-6995
Hale O Kapeka, Poipu B&B) (M) 742-6806
Hyatt Regency Kauai (Resort) (P) 800-233-1234
Kiahuna Plantation (Condos) (M) 800-367-8020
Koloa Landing Cottages (B&B) (C-M) 800-779-8773
Kuhio Shores (Condos) (C-M) 800-367-8022
Lawai Beach (Condos) (M-P) 800-367-8020
Nihi Kai Villas (Condos) (M) 800-367-8020
Poipu Crater Resort (Condos) (C) 800-367-8020
Poipu Kai Resort (Condos) (C-P) 800-367-8020
Poipu Shores (Condos) (M-P) 800-367-8020
Poipu Sands (Condos) (M-P) 800-367-8020
Sheraton Kauai (Resort) (P) 888-847-0208
Suite Paradise (Agent) (C-P) 800-367-8020
Whalers Cove (Condos) (P) 800-367-8020
Kauai Tree Houses, Kalaheo (B&B) (C)
    635-3945, 332-9045
**Waimea Plantation Cottages (Resort) (P)
    800-922-7860, 338-1625**

*All area codes are 808, unless otherwise noted

OAHU

WAIKIKI
Aloha Punawai (hotel) (C) 866-713-9694, 923-5211
Aqua Hotels and Resorts (10 properties) (M-P)
 866-406-2782) Aloha Surf (923-0222), Bamboo
 (922-9777), Palms (947-7256), Waikiki Wave
 (922-01262), The Equus Boutique Hotel (949-
 0061), Coconut Plaza (923-8828), Continental
 (922-2232), Island Colony (923-2345), Marina
 (942-7722), Ocean Tower Hotel (687-7700)
Aston Pacific Monarch (hotel) (M) 823-9805
Breakers (hotel) (C-M) 800-426-0494
Continental Surf (hotel) (C) 800-991-9228, 922-2232
Halekulani (resort) (P) 800-367-2343, 923-2311
Hawaii Polo Inn (hotel) (C) 949-0061
Hawaiian King (hotel) (C-M) 800-545-1948
Hilton Hawaiian Village (resort) (P)
 800-221-2424, 949-4321
Holiday Surf (condos) (C-M) 877-923-8488, 923-8488
Hyatt Regency Waikiki (resort) (P)
 800-554-9288, 923-1234
Ilima Hotel (M-P) 800-801-9366, 923-1877
Kahala Mandarin Oriental, Kahala, (resort) (P)
 800-367-2525, 739-8888
Kai Aloha Hotel (C-M) 923-6723
Marriott Waikiki Beach (resort) (P)
 800-367-5370, 922-6611
Moana Surfrider, Sheraton (resort) (P)
 888-488-3535, 922-3111
Manoa Valley Inn (M) 947-6019
Nahua Condominiums (C-M)
 800-655-6055, 923-5135
New Otani Kaimana Beach, Kapiolani, (resort)
 800-356-8264, 923-1555
Ocean Resort Hotel (hotel) (C-P)
 800-367-2317, 922-3861
Ohana Islander Waikiki (hotel) (M)
 800-462-6282, 923-7711
Ohana Waikiki Tower (hotel) (M)
 800-462-6262, 922-6424
Outrigger Waikiki on the Beach (resort) (P)
 800-688-7444-, 923-0711
Pacific Monarch (hotel) (M) 800-922-7866, 923-9805
Renaissance Ilikai Waikiki (resort) (P)
 800-245-4524, 949-3811
Royal Grove Hotel (C-M) 923-7691
Royal Hawaiian, Sheraton (resort) (P)
 888-488-3535, 923-7311
Sheraton Waikiki (resort) (P) 888-488-3515, 922-4422
W Honolulu Diamond Head (hotel) (P)
 877-946-8357, 922-3734
Waikiki Circle, Aston (hotel) (M)
 800-922-7866, 923-1571
Waikiki Grand (hotel) (C-M) 888-336-4368, 923-1814
Waikiki Joy Hotel, Aston (M) 800-922-7866, 923-2300
Waikiki Prince Hotel (C) 922-1544

WINDWARD, KAILUA, LANIKAI
Affordable Paradise B&B (agent) (C-M) 261-1693
Akamai, Kailua (B&B) (C) 261-2227
Beach Lane, Kailua (B&B) (C-M) 262-8286
Hawaiian Islands B&B (several) (M-P) 800-258-7895
Hawaii's Best Bed & Breakfast (agent) (M)
 800-262-9912

Hawaii's Hidden Hideaway, Lanikai (B&B) (C-M)
 877-443-3299
Laie Inn (motel) (M) 800-526-4562, 293-9282
Papaya Paradise (B&B)(C-M) 261-0316
Manu Mele (B&B) (C) 262-0016
Pat's Kailua Properties (agent) (C-P) 261-1653
Paradise Palms, Kailua (B&B) (C) 254-4234
Pillows in Paradise, Kailua (B&B) (C-M) B&B
 877-657-5745 262-8540

NORTH SHORE
Backpackers, Pupukea (C-M) 638-7838
Ironwoods, Sunset Beach (C) (studio) 293-2554
Keiki Beach Bungalows (C-P) 638-8229
Shark's Cove, Pupukea (B&B) (C) 888-883-0001
Sterman Realty (homes, condos) (C-P) 637-6200
Team Real Estate (homes, condos) (C-P)
 800-982-8602
Turtle Bay Condos (M) 293-2800
Turtle Bay Resort (P) 866-827-5327, 293-6000

WEST SIDE
Hawaiian Princess, Makaha (hotel) (M) 695-5604
JW Ihilani Resort (P) 800-626-4446, 679-0079
Sugar Cane Realty, Penny Dumont (M)
 696-5892, 497-3052
Listings for Makaha Valley Towers, Hawaiian Princess
Ola Properties, Ko Olina (condos) (M) 677-1063

MAUI

WAILEA
Maui Prince Hotel, Makena (P)
 800-321-6248, 874-1111
Four Seasons Resort (P) 874-8000
Grand Wailea Resort (P) 800-888-6100
Outrigger Wailea Resort (P)
 800-688-7444, 874-7981
Polo Beach Club, Wailea Elu'ua Village (Condos) (P)
 879-1595

KIHEI
Condominium Rentals Hawaii, (Agent) (C-P)
 800-367-5240)
Hale Pau Hana (Condos) (M-P) 800-367-6036
Kihei Beach Resort (Condos) 800-367-6034
Kihei Maui Vacations (Agent) (M-P) 800-541-6284
Kihei Surfside (Condos) (M-P) 800-367-5240
Maui Parkshore (Condos) (P) 879-1600
Maui Vista (Hotel) (M-P) 879-7966
Royal Mauian Resort (Hotel) (P) 879-1263
What a Wonderful World (B&B) 879-9103

NORTH KIHEI, MA'ALAEA
Aston Maui Lu (Hotel) (C-M) 800-321-2558
Kealia Resort (Hotel) (M-P) 879-0952
Kihei Holiday (Condos) (M-P) 879-9228
Koa Resort (Condos) 800-541-3060,
Luana Kai Resort (Hotel) (M) 879-1268
Maui Schooner (Condos) (M-P) 800-877-7976
Waipuilani (Condos) 879-1458
Kanai A Nalu (Condos) 244-3911
Ma'alaea Bay Rentals (Agent) (M-P) 800-367-6084
Ma'alaea Surf (Condos) (M-P) 800-423-7953
Noni Lani Cottages (C-M) 800-733-2688

Maui accommodations cont'd—

LAHAINA
Lahaina Inn (M) 800-669-3444, 572-5642
Lahaina Roads, Pu'upana (Condos) (M-P)
   800-669-6284
Lahaina Shores Resort (Suites) (P) 800-642-6284
Outrigger Aina Nalu (M) 800-462-6262
Pioneer Inn (Best Western) (M) 800-457-5457
Plantation Inn (M-P) 667-9225

KA'ANAPALI
Aston-Maui Ka'anapali Villas (Condos) (P)
   800-922-7866
Hyatt Regency (Hotel)(P) 800-233-1234, 661-1234
Ka'anapali Beach Hotel (P) 800-262-8450
Sheraton Maui Hotel (P) 800-782-9488
Westin Maui (Hotel) (P) 888-625-4949, 667-2525

KAHANA-KAPALUA
Hale Kai (Condos) (M-P) 800-446-7307
Hale Napili (Condos) (M) 669-6184
Honokeana (Condos) (M-P) 800-237-4948
Kahana Sunset (Condos) (M-P) 800-669-1488
Kahana Village (Condos) (P) 800-824-3065
Mauian Hotel on Napili (M) 800-367-5034
Maui Beachfront Rentals (Agent) (M-P) 888-661-7200
Napili Surf Beach Resort (M-P) 800-541-0638
Polynesian Shores (C) 800-433-6284
Ritz-Carlton Resort (P) 800-262-8440

KAHULUI-WAILUKU
Maui Seaside Hotel (C-M) 800-560-5552
Northshore Inn (C-M) 242-8999

PAIA, MAKAWAO
Inn at Mama's Fish House (M-P) 800-860-4852
Kua Cove Plantation (B&B) (M-P) 579-8988
Maui Vacation Properties (Agent) (C-P)
   800-782-6105
Spyglass House, Beach House (B&B) (C-P)
   800-475-6695

KULA
Kula Lodge (M) 800-233-1535, 878-1535
Malu Manu (cottage) (M) 888-878-6161
Peace of Maui (B&B) (M) 888-475-5045

HANA
Aloha Cottages (C-M) 248-8420
Ekena Bed & Breakfast (M) 248-7047
Hamoa Bay Bungalows (M) 248-7884
Hana Maui Travel Company (Agent) (M) 800-548-0478
Bamboo Inn, Hana Hale Inn (M) 248-7718
Hana Kai (Condos) (M) 800-346-2772
Hotel Hana Maui (P) 800-321-4262, 248-8211
Tradewinds Cottages (M-P) 248-8980
Tree Houses of Hana (M) 248-7241

LANAI
Hotel Lanai (M) 800-795-7211, 565-7211
Lanai City House (M) 565-6071
Manele Bay Hotel, Lodge at Koele (P), 800-321-4666,
   565-7300

MOLOKAI
Hotel Molokai (M) 553-5347
Kaluakoi Villas (Condos) (M) 800-525-1470
   800-367-5004, 552-2721
Kamalo Plantation (cottage, beach house) (C-M)
   558-8236
Molokai Friendly Isle Realty (Agent) 800-600-4158
Pu'umana-Pauwalu Beachfront Cottages (M)
   800-673-0520
Sheraton Molokai-Kaupoa Villas (M-P)
   877-726-4656, 660-2725

BIG ISLAND
KONA
Areca Palms, (B&B) Captain Cook (C-M)
   800-545-4390, 323-227
Black Bamboo, Kealakekua (M-P) 800-527-7789
Captains Suite-Bamboo Hideaway, Honauau (C-M)
   866-328-8686, 328-8687
A Hale Lanai (cottage), Holualoa (M) 530-583-6062
Holualoa Inn (breakfast) (M) 324-1121, 800-392-1812
Keauhou Beach Resort (M-P) 800-462-6262
King Kamehameha Hotel, Kailua (M-P) 923-4511,
   800-367-6060
Knutson & Associates (agent, condos) Kailua (M)
   329-6311, 800-800-6202
Kona Bali Kai Resort (condos) (M-P) 329-9381
Kona Magic Sands (condos) (C-M) 800-622-5348
Kona Surf Hotel, Kailua (C-M) 322-3411
Kona Tiki Hotel (breakfast) (C) 329-1425
The Lilikoi Vine, Kona mauka, (B&B) (C) 325-9856
Manago Hotel, Captain Cook (C) 323-2642
Nancy's Hideaway, Kona mauka (B&B) (M) 325-3132
Royal Kona Resort (M), 329-3111
Sea Village (condos) (M) 326-7434
Sheraton Keahou Resort (P) 888-488-3535, 930-4900
Tara Cottage, Kealakekua (M) 800-527-7789
Tommy Tinker's Pink House, Captain Cook (M)
   889-5584

SOUTH KOHALA
Fairmont Orchid Hawaii (P) 885-2000, 800-845-9905
Four Seasons Resort Hualalai (P) 325-8000
Hawaii Vacation Rentals (agent, Puako) (C-P)
   882-7000, 800-332-7081
Hawaiian Dream Properties, Waikaloa, 883-9660
Hilton Waikoloa Village (P) 886-1234, 800-445-8767
Kona Village Resort (P) 325-5555, 800-367-5290
MacArthur & Co. (agent), (M-P), Puako, 877-885-8285
Mauna Kea Beach Hotel (P) 882-7222, 800-882-6060
Mauna Lani Resort (P) 885-6622, 800-367-2323
Outrigger Waikoloa Beach (M-P) 800-922-5533

HAWI-WAIMEA
Cabin in the Treeline, mauka Hawi (M) 884-5105
Hawaii Palm Properties (agent), Hawi, 889-1295
Hawi Haven (cottage) (M) 884-5345
Jacaranda Inn, Waimea (M-P) 885-8813
Kamuela Inn (Waimea) (C-M) 885-4243,
Kohala Club Hotel, Kapaau (C) 889-6793
Kohala Village Inn, Hawi (C-M) 889-0404
Hale O Kohala (home), Kawaihae (M) 822-7022
Paniolo Cottage, Waimea (M) 866-399-5842
Tom Sherman House, Kapa'au (C-M) 889-0553

All area codes are 808, unless otherwise noted

Hilo-Hamakua
Shipman House (B&B), Hilo (M)
934-8002, 800-627-8447
Arnott's Lodge (hostel, rooms), Hilo (C) 969-7097
Hale Kukui Orchard Retreat (cottages), Honoka'a (M)
800-444-7130
Hawaii Naniloa Hotel (M), Hilo 800-367-5360
Hilo Hawaiian Hotel (M) 935-9361
Hotel Honoka'a Club (dorm, rooms) (C) 775-0678,
800-808-0678
Inn at Kulaniapia Falls (M) 966-6373, 888-838-6373
Luana Ola B&B Cottages, Honoka'a (M) 775-1150
Old Hawaii B&B, Hilo (C) 961-2816, 877-961-2816
Palms Cliff House (B&B) Honomu (P), 963-6076
Plantation Bungalow, Pepe'ekeo (C)
866-328-8686, 328-8687
Waipio Ridge Vacation Rental (cottage)
Honoka'a (M) 775-0603

Volcano
Hale Ohia Cottages (B&B) (M)
800-455-3803, 967-7986
Kilauea Lodge (includes breakfast) (M) 967-7366
Carson's Volcano Cottage (B&B) (M) 967-7683
Guesthouse at Volcano (cottages, B&B) (C-M)
967-7775
Holo Holo Inn (C) 967-7950
Volcano House (historic hotel on crater rim) (C-M)
967-7321
My Island Bed & Breakfast (C-M) 967-7216, 967-7110

Wood Valley, Na'alehu
The Big Island Cottage, Wood Valley (C-M)
888-256-4206
Macadamia Meadows B&B, Waiohinu (C-M)
929-8097, 888-929-8118
Pahala Plantation Cottages (C-P) 928-9811, 937-9965
SeaMountain at Punalu'u (condos) (M)
928-8301, 800-488-8301
Shirakawa Motel, Na'alehu (C) 929-7462
Wood Valley Temple & Retreat (C-M) 928-8539

Package Vacations
These companies also have an online presence. Also see online travel brokers—Orbitz, Expedia, Priceline, Hotels.com, Travelocity—and the websites of major airlines.

Pleasant Hawaiian Holidays 800-742-9244
Hawaii-Aloha.com 800-843-8777
Classic Vacations 800-835-1333
Hawaii Vacations 888-834-2524
Hawaii Travel Bureau 800-873-0370
Hawaii Travel Experts 800-672-5620
Panda Online 800-303-6702

Mainland Airlines
Hawaiian Airlines 800-367-5320
U.S. Airways 800-235-9292
American 800-433-7300
Alaska Airlines 800-252-7522
Continental 800-523-3273
Delta 800-221-1212
Northwest Airlines 800-225-2525
United 800-864-8331

Interisland Flights
Hawaiian Airlines is a major interisland carrier (see above).

Island Air 800-652-6541
Pacific Wings 567-6814 (No Kauai service)
Paragon 800-428-1231
Go! 888-435-9462

Interisland Ferry
Hawaii Superferry 877-443-3779
Service for individuals and automobiles from Honolulu to Maui. Service to the Big Island and Kauai scheduled to begin... sometime in the future.

Helicopters
Kauai, see page 148
Oahu and Maui, see page 149
Big Island, see page 150

Car Rental
Major companies also have pick-up locations in Waikiki, as well as the airport.

Alamo 800-327-9633
Avis 800-321-3712
Budget 800-527-0700
Dollar 800-800-4000
Enterprise 800-325-8007
Hertz 800-654-3011
National 800-227-7368
Thrifty 800-367-2277
Harper Car and Truck (4WD), 800-852-9993
(Big Island only)

SHUTTLES, TAXIS & PUBLIC TRANSPORTATION

KAUAI
Public Bus
The Kaua'i Bus, 241-6410
Shuttle-type buses cover the island.

Shuttles & Taxis
Any Time Shuttle 927-1120
Custom Limousine 246 6318
Kauai Limousine 245-4855
Kauai Taxi Company 246-9554
Brian's Taxi 245-6533
Akiko's Taxi 822-7588

OAHU
Public Bus
TheBus (route information, fares) 848-5555
   24-hour recorded information 296-1818
Waikiki Trolley 593-2822
Four different lines (pink, yellow, red, and blue) with open-air cars service greater Honolulu from Waikiki.

Taxis
Aloha State Cabs (wheelchairs) 847-3566
Charley's Taxi & Tours 531-1313
Handi-Cabs of the Pacific (wheelchairs) 524-3866
Pacific Taxi & Limousine 922-4545
Tradewinds Taxi & Tours 841-5555

Shuttle Buses
H&M, Co. 853-2338
Hawaii Super Transit 841-2928
Island Express Transport 944-1879
Oahu Airport Shuttle 834-8844
Reliable Shuttle and Tours 924-9292

MAUI
Public Buses
(run by Roberts) 871-4838

Ferries
Expeditions (to Lanai) 800-695-2624
Lahaina Cruise Company (to Molokai) 800-275-6969

Taxis and Shuttles
Island Wide Taxi 874-8294
Classy Taxi (Lahaina, airport) 665-0003
Maui Airport Taxi 877-0907
Sunshine Cabs 879-2220
Surf Taxi Maui 870-9974

BIG ISLAND
Public bus service
Hele-On Mass Transit 961-8744

Taxis & Shuttles
Speedishuttle 329-5433
Ioha Taxi (Kona side) 325-5448
Luana Limousine 326-5466
Kona Airport Taxi 329-7779
Hilo Harry's Taxi 935-7091

CAMPING

BEACH—Inexpensive camping permits are issued by both county and state. Many of the campgrounds are for weekends only, and most are closed one day a week for maintenance. Hawaiians like to party at beach camps, so expect company.

County beach park tent sites are fairly close together, often with covered pavilions, tables, showers, and restrooms that range in cleanliness from okay to sort of okay. It's not a good idea to leave valuables in an unattended tent; don't worry about any other crime than theft. It is a good idea to bring a larger tent to have the space during rain showers. Many state and county campgrounds normally do not allow camping on Wednesday and Thursday nights.

You'll need to bring only a minimum of equipment: Tent, lightweight sleeping bag, cook stove, and a minimum of utensils, centered around a Swiss Army knife. All of that goes easily into a duffel bag. When you get here, invest in a Styrofoam cooler, cook fuel, and gallon jugs of drinking water.

MOUNTAIN—Some great outdoor experiences are to be had camping at the high elevations in the islands—but then again, here you are in Hawaii freezing your butt off, so to speak. More gear is required. As long as you are aware of the campground's distance from the beach and palm trees, mountain camping can be an excellent choice.

RUSTIC ACCOMODATIONS—Hawaii is sprinkled with hostels, Euro-style inns, and rustic cabins that are either privately held or within public parks. Some of the offerings are not exactly cheap, when compared to deals you may get at a condo, private rental, or budget resort. The cheaper rustics are about $20 to $50 a night for a shared room or bath. Private-with-bath units range north of $50 and up to $100. So, if you elect to get a spiffier place at a budget resort, and save on food, you may be ahead of the game compared to getting a rustic cabin and then forking out for restaurants.

You need to shop it, and you have to be okay with a place that in some cases may be a little shabby and part of the elements, shall we say. The good news is many of the rustic accommodations are in awesome settings. And "a little shabby" doesn't mean you won't have all the creature comforts.

*All area codes are 808, unless otherwise noted

KAUA'I
Camping
Koke'e, Polihale, and Haena State Parks,
274-3444, 274-3446, 335-8405
Polihale is a huge sand beach, set on the west side beneath Napali ridges; maintenance has fallen off. Koke'e is chilly, set at about 4,000 feet; nice camping area on large, treed meadow, and good access to Waimea Canyon trails and lesser-used Napali ridge trails. North shore's Haena State Park is in a tropical setting, often frequented by locals and many tourists during the day.

Kalalau Trail, Napali Coast (backpacking), 245-4444,
274-3445
Koke'e Forest Reserves, including Waimea Canyon,
274-3433
County Beach Park Camping
241-4463, 241-4460
Best choices for visitors: Anini Beach Park, on the north shore near Princeville; Lydgate Park in Wailua; and Salt Pond Beach Park near Hanapepe.
Camp Naue 826-6418
YMCA North Shore, first come, first served; a beachside jewel. Has tent sites and dorm cabins.

Rustic Accommodations
Kaua'i International Hostel, Kapa'a, 823-6142
Right in town; recently refurbished.
Kahili Mountain Park, near Koloa 742-9921
Church-run cabins in beautiful setting. Some restrictions; go to www.kahilipark.org for current info.
Camp Sloggett, YMCA Koke'e State Park
(cabins and campsites) 245-5959
Koke'e Lodge Cabins 335-6061
Camp Naue, YMCA Haena 826-6419
Dorm cabins; friendly, beachfront setting

OAHU
Camping & Rustic Accommodations
For City & County of Honolulu beach parks 523-4525
For State Park sites call 587-0300.
Other phone numbers noted with listings.

Honolulu
Keaiwa Heiau State Recreation Area, Aiea
Easy access to central Oahu. Nice campground in gardenlike setting on 400 acres.
Sand Island State Recreation Area
At the end of an industrial area; open campground has a great view across the water at downtown Honolulu. Nice beach sunsets. Only open Friday, Saturday, and Sunday, and can be crowded.
Windward
Camp Kokokahi, Kaneohe 247-2124
A 10-acre conference center on Kaneohe Bay. Tent sites and lodge that accommodates groups.
Ahupua'a O Kahana State Park
Beautiful tropical setting, but it does get rain and the facilities are not well maintained.
Bellows Field Beach Park, Waimanalo
Campground with 50 sites in scenic forest with a great beach. Only open on three weekend nights and it gets heavy use.

Hau'ula Beach Park, Hau'ula
Close to highway in town, but not bad.
Ho'omaluhia Botanical Garden (county), Kaneohe
Magnificent setting below the pali on wide-open grassy camp area with a cooking pavilion. Only open three weekend nights.
Kokololio Beach Park, Laie
One of the prettiest beach parks in Hawaii. Just south of town, with 5 campsites. Nice beach with large treed landscaping.
Kualoa 'B' Regional Park
About 30 sites at a nice forest-and-beach country, with scenic mauka views. Historic park with Chinaman's Hat island offshore.
Swanzy Beach Park, Ka'a'awa
Located in quiet commercial area near Kaaawa.
Ahupua'a O Kahana State Park
A 5-acre lawn with trees fronts a seawall, and has 9 campsites. Only open on the three weekend days.
Waimanalo Beach Park
More than 20 sites on 40 beachfront acres. Scenic place, just out of town, with good swimming. Popular among locals.
Waimanalo Recreation Area (county)
Huge ironwood forest and long, scenic swimming beach make for good camping. Local guys may hang out, but the park has night security.

North Shore
Camp Erdman, Mokuleia 637-4615
A YMCA camp with clean cabins and tent sites set on the beach, a few miles west of Haleiwa. Cabins nicely spaced. Among the best beach cabins in Hawaii.
Hawaii Backpackers, Pupukea
888-628-8882, 638-7838
Accommodations range from $25 hostel rooms to private rooms with kitchen at $125 and up. No camping.
Kaiaka Bay Beach Park, Haleiwa
Quiet location, just outside of town. Pretty peninsula with ironwoods as huge beach trees. Night security. Better than decent.
Malaekahana State Recreation Area, Laie
Huge forested campground on a beautiful beach. Very scenic spot with nicely kept campground.
Malaekahana, Friends of Laie 293-1737
Yurts, funky cabins, and tent sites on the beach, right next to the state recreation area. Not exactly aesthetic.
Mokuleia Beach Park, Mokuleia
The park's 15 open sites are along the low dune of an undeveloped coast a few miles west of Haleiwa.
Surfhouse Hawaii, Haleiwa 637-7146
Walking distance from beaches. Tropical setting in town. Tent spaces, shared rooms and cabins, and private cabins with baths. Clean.

West Side
Camp Timberline, Kapolei 672-5441, 877-672-4386
Nonprofit school for kids set on 10 acres at 2,000 above Ewa. Several group cabins and a few tents. Safe and hang-loose with central-island location.
Camp Waianae, Waianae 595-7591
A Seventh Day Adventist camp in Waianae Valley with a half-dozen cabins and tent spaces. Kitchen and dining hall, along with a swimming pool.

Oahu camping cont'd—

Eisenhower Beach Park 684-5133
    Large campground in ironwood forest on the beach in Ewa between Nimitz and White Plains beach parks. No facilities, but some of the best beach camping in Hawaii. Operated jointly by the county and the military.

MAUI
Camping & Rustic Accommodations
County Beach Parks, camping, 270-7389
    Kanaha Beach Park, near Paia, is recommended.

STATE OF HAWAII
Department of Land and Natural Resources, 984-8110
    Parks, Camping 984-8109
Na Ala Hele Trails, 873-3508 or 3509
Waianapanapa Park caretaker, 248-4843
    Waianapanapa has excellent beach cabins, although rustic, near Hana. Polipoli is a high-elevation cabin, forest location. Pala'au and Waialua are great places on Molokai.

FEDERAL
Haleakala National Park 572-4400
    Kipahulu District 248-737
    *Cabins, tents, and backpacking 572-4400
    Holua, Kapalaoa, Paliku cabins are excellent; high-elevation, set within the valley of the volcano. Hosmer Grove Campground is pleasantly set in the forest at the entrance to the national park. Oheo Campground is on the Hana side of the national park, in a very scenic coastal setting.*

YMCA Camp Keanae 248-835
    Blue-water views from a open lawn on a bluff off the Hana Highway.
Banana Bungalow Hostel 244-5090 Wailuku
    Euro-style option for independent travelers.

BIG ISLAND
Camping
County Department of Parks and Recreation
    101 Pauahi Street, Suite 6, Hilo, HI, 96720
    961-8311, Kona, 887-3014, 327-3560.

State Department of Land and Natural Resources
    Division of State Parks, P. O. Box 936, Hilo, HI,
    96721. Phone: 974-4343, 974-6200, Wailoa
    Center. 933-0416, No fees for campgrounds.

Hawaii Volcanoes National Park P.O. Box 52, Hawaii
    National Park, HI, 96718
    985-6000, 985-6017. Two no-fee, no-reservation
    campgrounds are within the park.

Keokea Beach Park (county)
    Set on a remote bay, with good access of Pololu Valley. Pavilion, lawn, showers, drinking water. Popular with local community, particularly on weekends.
Kapa'a Beach Park (county)
    Beautifully situated on a rugged Kohala coastline. Pavilion with a whale-watching view. No drinking water.

Mahukona Beach Park (county)
    Nice lawn camping with good snorkeling on Kohala coast. Large pavilion with tables. Shower, but no drinking water. Doesn't get a lot of local use, but fairly popular among travelers.
Spencer Beach Park (county)
    Beautiful stone pavilion, drinking water, indoor showers. Shaded large camping area next to swimming beach and a short walk to excellent snorkeling beach. Gets a lot of use. Near Pu'ukohola Heiau.
Kohanaiki Coastal Park (private, 334-9700)
    Newly developed north Kona park at site of Pinetrees surfing beach is available on long list of holidays. Need 4WD to get the last .75-mile.
Ho'okena Beach Park (county)
    'Cozy' beachside camping at this popular park, the closest to Kailua-Kona. Rest rooms, showers, picnic tables.
Miloli'i Beach Park (county)
    Not many tourists spend the night in Miloli'i, and the campground feels more like a day-use area. More privacy on weekdays.
Manuka State Park (state)
    Beautiful native forest, midway between Kona and Hawaii Volcanoes. Set at about 2,000 feet, cooler but not cold. One of the more woodsy, quiet campgrounds.
Whittington Beach Park (county)
    Remotely located on east coast above South Point, this is one of the least used county parks, in spite of its scenic charms. Restrooms, showers, and pavilion, but no drinking water.
Punalu'u Beach Park (county)
    Set on a hillside next to the Big Island's most popular black sand beach. Wind can be a factor. Locals like the pavilion for parties, particularly on weekends.
Namakani Paio Campground (federal)
    Located 3 miles west of the entrance to Hawaii Volcanoes National Park on Highway 11. Nice lawn surrounded by lush forest. Full facilities. Can be damp and chilly, set at 4,000-feet. Fairly popular among tourists.
Kulanaokuaiki Campground (federal)
    Located within Hawaii Volcanoes National Park, on Hilina Pali Road. Will be warmer and drier (at 2,700 feet) than Namakani Paio, but also in an arid setting. Usually quiet and private.
Mackenzie State Recreation Area (state)
    Set within a huge coastal ironwood grove along the lush Puna coast. Has picnic area, pavilion, and rest rooms, but no drinking water. Frequented by fishermen, mostly on weekends, and not many tourists.
Kolekole Beach Park (county)
    In a lovely jungle gorge, fairly close to Hilo and very near Akaka Falls State Park. Nice lawn with pavilion, picnic facilities, and showers. Gets local action, particularly on weekends, due to proximity to Hilo.
Laupahoehoe Point Beach Park (county)
    Beautiful, well-kept coastal setting. Nice lawn area with plenty of trees and full facilities. On weekend evenings, locals like to gather at the park, but the place usually is not overcrowded with campers.
Kalopa State Park (state)
    Among the best sites, set around a large meadow in a native forest. Full facilities. Can be damp and chilly, at 2,000 feet. Usually uncrowded and quiet. Also has cabins, which are listed below.

Rustic Lodging

Hapuna Beach State Park (state)
About a half-dozen A-frames, perhaps in disrepair, are nicely spaced on an arid hillside above the island's most-popular beach. A large communal cooking pavilion is nearby. Rent is about $40.

Manago Hotel (private) 323-2642
Basic but hardly rustic, the Manago is a Big Island classic. Views of Keulakekua Bay. Easy Kona access from Captain Cook. Japanese restaurant attached, and stores of the town are nearby. Deluxe rooms for $50 and under.

Shirakawa Motel (private) 929-7462
South Island's version of the Manago, located in jungle greenery on the outskirts of Na'alehu. Clean, quiet rooms for under $40.

Wood Valley Temple (private) 928-8539
Rustic, private rooms and a share-kitchen on the lovely grounds of an internationally known Buddhist retreat. Rooms are around $50.

Namakani Paio Cabins (private) 967-7321
Ten cabins next to the campground, 3 miles west from the Hawaii Volcanoes National Park entrance. Communal rest rooms and showers. Bedding included, but it gets chilly, so bring an extra blanket. About $40 gets you a cabin. Operated by Volcano House Hotel.

Holo Holo Inn (private) 967-7950
To call the modest Holo an Inn is generous, but they have clean rooms, in Volcano. Dorms are under $20, and privates are about $50.

Kulana Retreat (private) 985-9055
Kulana is an artist retreat with cabins, rooms, and camping. Prices range from $15 to $30. Near the national park and Volcano Village restaurants, in the ohia-and-tree fern birdlands.

Kalani Retreat (private) 965-7828, 800-800-6886
A range of possibilities —$20 campsites, $60 shared rooms, and cabins ranging from $100 to $200. All set on 100-plus verdant acres on a lovely part of the Puna Coast.

Arnott's Lodge (private) 969-7097
Enterprising Aussie Doug Arnott has tent spaces for $9 and private rooms for about $60—with lots of options in between. Just ask. Walking distance to good beaches in Hilo. Shuttle service from the airport, plus cross-island excursions. You're bound to meet interesting people, many of them Euro-style and student travelers.

Kalopa Native Forest State Park
Large cabins on the manicured grounds of the park, set at 2,000 feet. Can be chilly and damp, but these cabins are a find. Cabins range from $30 to $50 a night.

MUSEUMS & GALLERIES

All listings are recommended.
Boldfaced = top 20 Best Of listing
• = top 5 listing

KAUAI

•**Waioli Mission House, Hanalei 245-3202**
Kaua'i Museum, Lihue 245-6931
Grove Farm Homestead, Lihue 245-3202
Gay & Robinson Sugar Plantation Tours, Waimea 335-2824
Koke'e Natural History Museum, Koke'e 335-9975
Kaua'i Children's Discovery Museum, Kapa'a 823-8222

OAHU

•**Bishop Museum and Learning Center 847-3511**
•**Honolulu Academy of Arts 532-8700**
•**Hawaii Maritime Center 536-6373**
U.S. Army Museum, Ft. DeRussy 438-2821, 438-2822
North Shore Surf & Cultural Museum 637-8888
Mission Houses Museum 531-0481
Queen Emma Summer Palace 595-3167, 595-3603
Tropic Lightning Museum 655-0438
Hawaii State Art Museum 586-0900
USS Bowfin Submarine Museum & Park 423-1342
Bishop Hilton Kalia Tower annex 947-4321
The Contemporary Museum 526-0232
Falls of Clyde 523-6151

MAUI

Bailey House Museum 244-3326
Hale Pa'ahao prison 667-1985
Baldwin Museum and Courthouse 661-3262
Wo Hing Museum 661-4020
Alexander & Baldwin Sugar Museum 871-8058
Carthaginian 661-8521
Hana Cultural Center 248-8622

BIG ISLAND

Eva Parker Woods Cottage, Mauna Lani 885-6622
Volcano Art Center 967-8222, 967-7565
Hulihe'e Palace, Kona, 329-1877, 329-9555
Thomas A. Museum Jaggar, Volcano 985-6000
Kona Coffee Living History Farm 323-2006
Isaacs Art Center, Waimea 885-5884
Kaupulehu Cultural Center 323-8520
Kona Historical Society 323-3222
Pacific Tsunami Museum, Hilo 935-0926
Onizuka Space Center, Kona 329-3441
Lyman House Museum, Hilo 935-5021
Memories of Hawaii-Plantation Museum, Honomu 961-0024
Onizuka Center for Astronomy, Hilo 961-2180
Parker Ranch Historic Homes 885-5433, 885-0554

ATTRACTIONS & VISITOR CENTERS

All listings are recommended.
Boldfaced = top 20 Best Of listing
• = top 5 listing

KAUAI
•Kilauea Point National Wildlife Refuge
828-1413, 828-0383, 246-2860
Smith's Fern Grotto Cruise, Wailua 821-6892
Kilohana Plantation, Lihue 245-5608
Gay & Robinson Sugar Plantation Tours 335-2824
Kaua'i Coffee Company Visitors Center
800-545-8605, 335-5497
Guava Kai Plantation, Kilauea 828-6121
Kaua'i Sunshine Markets 241-6390
Fort Elizabeth State Park Waimea, 245-4444
Kamokila Hawaiian Village, Wailua 823-0559

OAHU
•USS Arizona Memorial, Pearl Harbor
422-0561, 422-2771
•Polynesian Cultural Center 800-367-7060,
233-3333, 293-3305
•Iolani Palace 522-0832
Hawaii's Plantation Village 677-0110
Waikiki Aquarium 923-9741
Shangri La (Doris Duke's) 866-385-3849, 532-3853
Chinatown, Oahu Market, 841-6924,
Maunakea Marketplace, 524-3409
Ali'iolani Hale (Judiciary Center) 539-4999
Aloha Stadium Swap Meet 486-6704
Aloha Tower Marketplace 566-2337
Duke's Canoe Club 922-2268
Hawaiian Railway Society 681-5461
Honolulu Zoo 971-7174, 971-7171
HURL (Hawaii Undersea Research Lab) 956-9772
Kualoa Ranch 237-7321
Sea Life Park 259-7933
Tropical Farms, Ali'i Tour 877-505-6887
USS Missouri 973-2494, 423-2263
Ala Moana Shopping Center 955-9517
Buffalo's Big Board Surfing Classic 668-9712
Dole Plantation 621-8408
Dolphin Quest 739-8918
Hawaiian Waters 674-9283
Oceanarium, Waikiki 922-1233
Sunset on the Beach (movies) 923-1094
Top of Waikiki 923-3877

MAUI
•Maui Ocean Center 270-7000
Haleakala Visitors Center-Red Hill Pavilion 572-4400
Ulupalakua Ranch-Tedeschi Winery
878-1266, 878-6058
Humpback Whale National Marine
Sanctuary 800-831-4888
Maui Swap Meet 877-3100, 242-0240
Sugar Cane Train 661-0089
Hasegawa General Store, Hana 248-8231, 248-7079
Kaupo Store 248-8054
Lahaina Cannery Mall, 661-5304

BIG ISLAND
•Mauna Kea Observatories-Onizuka Center
935-7606, 969-4892
•Kilauea Visitors Center, Hawaii Volcanoes National
Park, 985-6000, Volcano House 967-7321
Mokupapapa Discovery Center for Remote
Hawaii's Reefs, Hilo 933-8195
Royal Kona Coffee 847-3600, Ueshima Coffee
Company 888-822-5662
Bay View Farm 328-9658, Blue Sky 322-1700
Hilo Farmers Market 933-1000
Imiloa Astronomy Center, Hilo 969-9700
Mauna Loa Macadamias Visitors Center, Hilo
888-628-6556
Onizuka Space Center, Kona Airport 329-3441
Panaewa Rainforest Zoo (county), Hilo 959-7224,
959-9233
Volcano Winery 967-7772

HAWAIIAN TEMPLES & ANCIENT SITES

KAUAI
Department of Land and Natural Resources 742-7033

OAHU
Department of Land and Natural Resources 587-0077

MAUI
State Historic Preservation Division 243-5169
Pi'ilanihale Heiau 248-8912
County Culture & Arts 961-8706

BIG ISLAND
Mo'okini Heiau 591-1170
Hawaii Volcanoes National Park 985-6000
Kaloko-Honokohau National Historic Park 329-6881
Pu'uhonua o Honaunau National Historic
Park 328-2288
Pu'ukohola Heiau National Historic Site 882-7218
Kealakowa'a Heiau, Kona 329-7286
Kona Village Petroglyphs 325-5555
Lapakahi State Historical Park
882-6207, 889-5566

*All area codes are 808, unless otherwise noted

BOTANICAL GARDENS

All listings are recommended.
Boldfaced = top 20 Best of Listing
• = top 5 listing

KAUAI
•Allerton National Tropical Botanical Garden
742-2623, 742-2433
•Na Aina Kai Botanical Gardens, Kilauea 828-0525
•Limahuli National Tropical Botanical Garden,
Haena 826-1053
Smith's Tropical Paradise, Wailua 821-6895
McBryde National Tropical Botanical Garden
742-2623, 742-2433
Moir Gardens, Kiahuna Plantation, Poipu 742-6411

OAHU
•Lyon Arboretum 988-0456
•Waimea Valley Audubon Center 638-9199
Ho'omaluhia Botanical Garden 233-7323
Koko Crater Botanical Garden 522-7060
Foster Botanical Garden 522-7066, 522-7065
Wahiawa Botanical Garden 621-7321
Senator Fong's Plantation Gardens 239-6775
Liliuokalani Botanical Garden 522-7060

MAUI
Keanae Arboretum 984-8109
Kahanu National Tropical Botanical Garden
248-8912, 332-7374
Garden of Eden 572-9899
Kepaniwai Heritage Gardens 270-7230,
Hawaii Nature Center 244-6500
Iao Valley Botanical Garden 984-8109, 587-0300
Ali'i Kula Lavender 878-3004, 878-8090
Kula Botanical Garden 878-1715
Maui Nui Botanical Garden 249-2798

BIG ISLAND
•Hawaii Tropical Botanical Garden, Hilo 964-5233
World Botanical Gardens, Hilo 963-5427
Liliuokalani Gardens, Hilo 961-8707
Amy Greenwell Ethnobotanical Garden,
Captain Cook 323-3318
Panaewa Rainforest Zoo (county), Hilo
959-7224, 959-9233
Akatsuka Orchid Gardens, Volcano 888-967-6669
Hilo Forestry Arboretum 974-4221

CHURCHES & HOLY PLACES

All listings are recommended.
Boldfaced = top 20 Best Of listing
• = top 5 listing

KAUAI
•Waioli Hui'ia Church, Hanalei 826-6253
88 Holy Places of Kobo Diashi 822-5942
Kaua'i Hindu Monastery, Kapa'a 822-3012, 822-3152
St. Raphael's Catholic Church, Koloa 742-1845

OAHU
•Byodo-In Temple 239-9844, 239-4724
•Punchbowl-National Memorial Cemetery of
the Pacific 532-3720
Mormon Temple Visitors Center 293-9297
Royal Mausoleum 536-7602, 587-2590
Kawaiahao Church 522-1333

MAUI
•Huialoha Church, Kaupo 248-8054
•St. Augustine Shrine-St. Gabriel Church 575-2601
'Ihi'ihiolehowaona Kaua Church, Keanae (n/a)
Kipahulu Church (St. Paul's) 248-8030
Keawala'i Congregational Church, 879-5557
Kaulanapuewo Church, Huelo 572-1850
Jodo Mission, Lahaina 661-0640
Francis Xavier Mission 244-3284
St. Joseph Church, Kaupo 248-8030
Church of the Holy Ghost, Kula 878-1261

BIG ISLAND
Painted (St. Benedict's) Church,
Kealakekua 328-2227
Mokuaikaua Church, Kona 329-1589
Wood Valley Temple 928-8539
Kahikolu Congregational Church 328-8110

Tours & Outfitters

KAUA'I

Surfing
Hanalei Surf Company 826-9000
Learn To Surf 826-7612
Lessons, rentals, island-wide
Nukomoi Surf Company, Poipu 742-8019
Rentals, lessons, surf shop
Tamba Surf Company, Kapa'a 823-6942
Rentals, surf shop, lessons
Hawaiian School of Surfing 652-1116
Learn from surfing legend Titus Kinimaka
Dr. Ding's Westside Surf Shop, Hanapepe 335-3805

Cruises & Snorkeling
Captain Andy's 800-535-0830
Napali coast specialsts; well trained
Holoholo Charters, Port Allen
800-848-6130, 335-0815
Snorkeling Niihau and other excursions
Napali Explorer, Waimea 877-335-9909, 338-9999
Sea Sport Divers, Poipu 742-9303, *tours, lessons*
Snorkel Bob's, Kapa'a 823-9433,
Koloa, 742-2206, *rentals*

Sightseeing
Roberts of Hawaii 800-831-5541, 245-9101
Kauai Island Tours 245-4777
Polynesian Adventure Tours 246-0122

Hiking
Princeville Ranch Adventures 826-7669
Also zipline and kayak, waterfall swim
Island Enchantment 823-0705
Also snorkeling
Kaua'i Nature Tours, Poipu 888-233-8365

Helicopters
Air Kauai 800-972-4666, 246-4666, 647-4646
Reliable and smooth operation
Blue Hawaiian 800-745-2583, 245-5800
Hard to beat these guys; they do three islands
Safari Helicopters 800-326-3356

Horseback Riding
CJM Country Stables, Poipu 742-6096
Esprit De Corps Academy, Kapa'a 822-4688
Princeville Ranch Stables 826-6777
Silver Falls Ranch, Kilauea 828-6718
Exotic setting wet forests beneath green ridgetops

Kayaking
Kayak Kaua'i, Hanalei 800-437-3507, 826-9844
Also surfing, beach cruiser bikes, custom hiking
Kalapaki Beach Boys-True Blue 246-6333
Also surfing, windsurfing, cruises, deep sea fishing
Aloha Canoes and Kayaks, Nawiliwili 246-6804
Napali Kayak Tours, Hanale 826-6900
Specialize in coast camping
Outfitters Kaua'i, Nawiliwili and Poipu 742-9667
Wailua River Kayak, Wailua 822-5795, 639-6332
Family operation; guides to Secret Falls

Bicycling
Kaua'i Cycle and Tour, Kapa'a 821-2115
Pedal 'n Paddle, Hanalei 826-9069
Also kayaks, snorkeling, boogie boards, camping
Bicycle Downhill, Waimea 742-7421,
Tours, Waimea Canyon
Bike Doktor, Hanalei 826-7799
Rentals, sales, service

ATV
Kaua'i ATV Tours 877-707-7088
Kipu Ranch Adventures 246-9288
Robinson Family Adventures 335-2824
A huge ranch that dates from the time of Kamehameha; they also own Niihau (island).

Golf
Kalapaki Lagoon 800-634-6400
Grove Farm Golf Course at Puakea 245-8756
Kiahuna Golf Club, Poipu 742-9595
Kukuiolono Golf Course, Kalaheo, 332-9151
Poipu Bay Resort Golf Course 800-858-6300
Princeville Golf Club 800-826-1105
Wailua Golf Club 241-6666

OAHU

Surfing
DCX Surf School, Waikiki 926-1414
Hans Hedemann Surf School 924-7778
Hawaiian Fire Surf School 384-8855
Hawaiian Watersports 255-4352
Also kite-boarding, windsurfing
Town & Country Surf Shop 483-8383
Sunset Suzy 781-2693
Surf-N-Sea, Haleiwa 800-899-7873
Surf Hawaii 4 U, North Shore 295-1241
Hale Nalu Surf Company, Makaha 696-5897
Also bike rentals

Cruises & Snorkeling
Aloha Dive, Honolulu 395-5922
AquaZone, Waikiki 923-3483
Breeze Hawaii, Waikiki 735-1857
Snorkel Bob's 735-7954
Deep Ecology, Haleiwa 800-578-3992
Well respected in the North Shore; also involved in preservation efforts
West Side Specialty Tours, Waianae 306-7273

Sightseeing
Roberts of Hawaii 800-831-5541
Discover Hawaii Hidden Tours 946-4432
Polynesian Adventure Tours 833-3000
E Noa Tours 866-268-7459

Hiking
Na Ala Hele trails (hikes, permits)
973-9782, www.hawaiitrails.org
Hawaiian Trail & Mountain Club 674-1459, 377-5442
The Nature Conservancy 537-4508
Hike Oahu 955-4453
Oahu Nature Tours 924-2473
Mauka Makai Excursions 896-0596

*All area codes are 808, unless otherwise noted

Helicopters
Makani Kai 877-255-8532, 834-5813
Paradise Helicopters 888-349-7888
Genesis Aviation 840-1111

Horseback Riding
Happy Trails, Pupekea 638-7433
Kualoa Ranch, Windward 237-8515

Kayaking
Kailua Sailboards & Kayaks 262-2555
Two Good Kayaks 262-5656
> Both good choices to rent kayak for the short paddle to the tiny Windward islands

Bicycling
Big Kahuna, Waikiki (rentals) 924-2736
Boca Hawaii, Waikiki (rentals) 591-9839
Coconut Cruisers, Waikiki (rentals) 924-1644
Bike Hawaii, John Alford 877-682-7433, 734-4214
> Bike tours, snorkel, hike; this is the guy you want for off-road and touring adventures
Country Cycles, North Shore 638-8866
> Specialize in renting cruisers for the bike path to check out the surf scene

ATV
Kualoa Ranch 237-7321
> Large ranch is the site of movie and commerical sets

Golf
Ala Wai Golf Course 733-7387
Hawaii Country Club, Waihiawa 621-5654
Hawaii Kai Championship Golf Course 395-2358
Hawi Prince Golf Club, Ewa 944-4567
Kapolei Golf Course 674-2227
Ko Olina Golf Club 676-5300
Ko'olau Golf Course, Windward 236-4653
Luana Hills Country Club, Windward 262-2139
Makaha Resort Gold Club 695-7519
Moanalua Golf Club 839-2311
Turtle Bay Resort, Palmer Course 293-8574

MAUI
Surfing
Big Kahuna 875-6395
> Also snorkel, kayaks
Goofy Foot, Lahaina 244-9283, 229-6737
Hawaiian Style Surf, Kihei 874-0110
Maui Waveriders, Kihei 875-4761
Outrageous Adventures, Lahaina 1-877-339-1400
Soul Surfing Maui 870-7873
Surf Dog Maui, Lahaina, 250-7873

Windsurfing
Action Sports Maui 871-5857
Hawaiian Sailboarding Techniques
  (HST) 871-5423
Hi-Tech Surf Sports 871-7766
Maui Sailing Center 870-2554
Maui Windsurf Company 877-4696
Second Wind 877-7467

Cruises & Snorkeling
Maui Dive Shop 879-1775; Kihei, 879-3388,
  879-1533; Kahana, 661-6166, 669-3800;
  Ka'anapali, 661-5117; Lahaina, 661-5388;
  Ma'alaea, 244-5514
> A large outfit that has not lost the personal touch.
B&B Scuba 875-2861
Blue Dolphin 662-0075
Ed Robinson's Diving (scuba) 800-635-1273, 879-3584
Ehukai Catamaran, Lanai (also whale watch) 871-0626
Hawaiian Rafting Adventures 661-7333
Lahaina Divers (scuba) 800-998-3483, 667-7496
Maui Undersea Adventures 874-2276
Seafire, Kihei 879-2201
Trilogy 888-MAUI-800
Pacific Whale Foundation 800-942-5311, 249-8811
Captain Commando 661-8299
Explorer, Lahaina 661-5550
Gemini, Lahaina 669-0508
Pride of Maui 242-0955
Teralani, Ka'anapali 661-0365

Sightseeing
Aikina Aloha Tours 879-2828
Roberts of Hawaii 800-831-5541
Polynesian Adventure Tours 877-4242
Temptation Tours 800 817 1234
Ekahi Tours 888-292-2422

Hiking
Haleakala National Park 572-4400
Hawaii Nature Center, Iao Valley 244-6500
The Nature Conservancy 572-7849
Kapalua Nature Society (Pu'u Kukui hike),669-0244
Maui Eco-Adventures 661-7720
> Also snorkel, kayak
Hike Maui 866-325-6284
> They'll get you off the beaten track to cool places

Helicopters
Blue Hawaiian 800-745-2583, 871-8844
Air Maui 877-238-4922
Sunshine Helicopters 866-501-7738

Horseback Riding
Adventures on Horseback, Makawao 242-7445
Ironwood Ranch, Kapalua 669-4991
Haleakala on Horseback 888-349-7888
Horse Whisperer, Makawao 572-6211
Makena Stables 879-0244
Mendes Ranch, Kahakuloa 871-5222
Oheo Stables 667-2222
Pony Express Tours, Kula 667-2200

Kayaking
Hana Maui Sea Sports 248-7711, 264-9566
Keli'i's Kayak Tours 874-7652
Kihei Canoe Club (visitors welcome) 879-5505
Makena Kayak 879-8426
Maui Ultra Dive, Kihei 891-1442
Ocean Activities, Wailea 875-1234
Pacific Coast Kayak 879-2391
South Pacific Kayaks, Kihei
  800-776-2326, 875-4848

Bicycling
Aloha Bike Tours 800-749-1564, 249-0911
Cruiser Phil's 893-2332
Emerald Island Bicycle Rides 800-565-6615, 573-1278
Haleakala Bike Company 888-922-2453, 575-9575
Hawaii Downhill 893-2332
Maui Downhill 800-535-2453, 871-2155
Mountain Riders Bike Tours 800-706-7700
Upcountry Cycles 800-373-1678, 573-2888

ATV
Haleakala ATV Tours 661-0388

Golf
Dunes at Maui Lani 873-0422
Ka'anapali Tournament Golf Course 661-3691
Kapalua Plantation Golf Course 877-527-2582
  Also The Bay and The Village courses
Makena Golf Club, North & South 879-3344
Maui Country Club 877-0616
Pukalani Country Club 572-1314
Waiehu Municipal Golf Course 270-7400
Wailua Golf Clubs, Blue 875-5115,
  Emerald & Gold 875-7450

BIG ISLAND
Surfing
Kona Boys 328-1234
  Also snorkel, kayaks
Hawaii Lifeguard Surf Instructors 866- 324-0442
Ocean Eco Tours, Kona 324-7873
Aloha Girls Surf Camp 896-7656

Cruises & Snorkeling
Adventures in Paradise 866-824-2337
Big Island Divers 800-488-6068, 329-6068
Big Island Water Sports Snuba 326-7446
Body Glove Cruises 800-551-8911, 326-7122
Captain Zodiac 329-3199
Dolphin Discoveries 322-8000
Fair Wind (Cook Monument) 322-2788
Hawaiiana Boat Rentals 322-8006
Kamanu Charters (catamaran) 329-2021
Kohala Divers, Kawaihae 882-7774
Kona Boat Rentals 326-9155
Kona Honu Divers, Kailua, 324-4668
Manta Ray Dives of Hawaii 325-1687
Planet Ocean Watersports, Hilo 935-7277
Red Sail Sports 886-2876
Sea Quest Raft & Snorkel, Keauhou 329-RAFT
South Kona Snorkeling 328-1609

Sightseeing
Roberts of Hawaii 800-831-5541
Polynesian Adventure Tours, Hilo 969-3208,
  Kona 329-8008
Arnott's Lodge & Hiking Adventures 969-7097
  Also hikes; based in Hilo
Mauna Kea Summit Adventures 888-322-2366
Hawaii Forest & Trail 331-8505, 800-464-1993,
  334-9555

Hiking
Hawaii Forest & Trail 331-8505, 800-464-1993,
  334-9555
  The Big Island's premier outdoor tour company
Hawaiian Walkways 800-457-7759

Helicopters
Blue Hawaiian 800-745-2583, 961-5600
Safari 326-3356

Horseback Riding
Ainahou Ranch, Waimea 985-7373
Dahana Ranch, Waimea 885-0057
Kapapala Ranch, Volcano 968-6585
Kealia Ranch, Honaunau, 328-8744
Kohala Na'alapa Stables 889-0022
Mauna Kea Beach Stables 885-4288
Paniolo Adventures Waimea 889-5354
Waipio on Horseback 775-7291
Waipio Ridge Stables 877-757-1414

Kayaking
Adventures in Paradise, Kona 866-824-2337
Aloha Kayak, Kona 877-322-1444
Hawaii Pack & Paddle, Captain Cook 328-8911
Ocean Safaris Kayak, Kona 326-4699
Kohala Kayak 866-547-5861

ATV
Top of Waipio 877-757-1414
ATV Outfitters, Kapa'au 889-6000
Kealia Ranch, South Kona 328-8777
Parker Ranch 885-7655

Bicycling
Big Island Mountain Bike Assoc. 961-4452
Dave's Bikes 329-4522
Hawaiian Pedals 329-2294
Kona Coast Cycling Tours 877-592-2453
Mauna Kea Mountain Bikes 888-682-867

Golf
Hapuna Golf Course 880-3000
Hilton Waikoloa Seaside 886-1234
Big Island Country Club 325-5044
Francis H. I'i Brown (Mauna Lani)
  North & South Courses 885-6655
Waikoloa Beach Course 886-6060
Waikoloa Kings' Course 886-7888
Waimea Country Club 885-8777
Kona Country Club 322-2595
Makalei Hawaii Club 325-6625
Hilo Municipal Course, 959-7711
Naniloa Country Club 935-3000
Hamakua Country Club 775-7244
Discovery Harbor 929-7353
Sea Mountain Golf Course 928-6222
Volcano Country Club 967-7331

Index

Your Notes

Aloha

Bianca Soriano
Halau Na Pua 'O Uluhaimalama

For publisher-direct savings to individuals and groups, and for book-trade orders, please contact:

DIAMOND VALLEY COMPANY, Publishers
89 Lower Manzanita Drive
Markleeville, CA 96120

Phone-fax 530-694-2740
www.trailblazertravelbooks.com
email: trailblazertravebooks@gmail.com

All titles are also available through Amazon, WalMart.com and all major Internet sites, as well as Barnes and Noble, Borders, and most independent bookstores. Please contact the publisher with comments, corrections, and suggestions. We value your readership!

Most images in Trailblazer Travel Books are available for licensing from Diamond Valley Company. Please e-mail your request to trailblazertravelbooks@gmail.com.

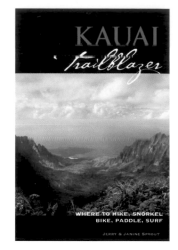

TRAILBLAZER TRAVEL BOOK SERIES:

NO WORRIES HAWAII
A Vacation Planning Guide for
Kauai, Oahu, Maui, and the Big Island
ISBN-10: 0-9670072-9-1
ISBN-13: 978-0-9670072-9-8

KAUAI TRAILBLAZER
Where to Hike, Snorkel, Bike, Paddle, Surf
ISBN-10: 0-9670072-1-6
ISBN-13: 978-0-9670072-1-2

MAUI TRAILBLAZER
Where to Hike, Snorkel, Paddle, Surf, Drive
ISBN-10: 0-9670072-4-0
ISBN-13: 978-0-9670072-4-3

HAWAII THE BIG ISLAND TRAILBLAZER
Where to Hike, Snorkel, Surf, Bike, Drive
ISBN-10: 0-9670072-5-9
ISBN-13: 978-0-9670072-5-0

OAHU TRAILBLAZER
Where to Hike, Snorkel, Surf
From Honolulu to the North Shore
ISBN-10: 0-9670072-8-3
ISBN-13: 978-0-9670072-8-1

ALPINE SIERRA TRAILBLAZER
Where to Hike, Ski, Bike, Fish, Drive
From Tahoe to Yosemite
ISBN-10: 0-9786371-0-0
ISBN-13: 978-0-9786371-0-1

GOLDEN GATE TRAILBLAZER
Where to Hike, Walk, Bike
In San Francisco and Marin
ISBN-10: 0-9670072-7-5
ISBN-13: 978-0-9670072-7-4

"In layout, design, and content, Trailblazers are the very model of what a user-friendly travel guide should be."

—MIDWEST BOOK REVIEW

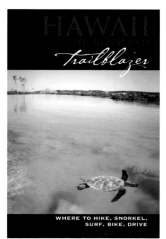

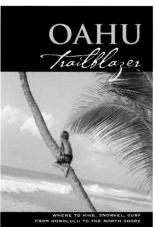